D0627121

BELIEVING THE PROMISE

BELIEVING THE PROMISE

*Daily Devotions for
Following Your Dreams*

HEATHER WHITESTONE McCALLUM

With Carolyn Curtis

DOUBLEDAY
New York   London   Toronto   Sydney   Auckland

PUBLISHED BY DOUBLEDAY
a division of Random House, Inc.
1540 Broadway, New York, New York 10036

DOUBLEDAY and the portrayal of an anchor with a dolphin are
trademarks of Doubleday, a division of Random House, Inc.

BOOK DESIGN BY JENNIFER ANN DADDIO

Library of Congress Cataloging-in-Publication Data

Whitestone McCallum, Heather.
Believing the promise: daily devotions for following
your dreams
Heather Whitestone McCallum. — 1st ed.
p. cm.
I. Whitestone McCallum, Heather.   2. Meditations.
I. Title.
BV4811.W58   1999
242′.2—dc21   98-48835
CIP

ISBN 0-385-49507-2

First Edition

1   3   5   7   9   10   8   6   4   2

ACKNOWLEDGMENTS

First, I want to thank God for blessing me with the opportunity to spread the Good News through this book. I am still humbled that God has given an imperfect Christian the opportunity to touch the lives of so many people throughout the world.

This book was a team effort in many respects, and I want to thank those people who have been part of my support team. I want to thank my agent at the William Morris Agency, Claudia Cross. Claudia was instrumental in the production of my first book, *Listening with My Heart*, and she has helped me in more ways than I can describe in this short space. I also want to thank my editor at Doubleday, Trace Murphy. Trace has been the guiding force behind my literary work thus far, and he is largely responsible for the wonderful flow of my last two books. Producing a book takes an enormous effort and the work of many hands, and I want to thank all of the wonderful people at Doubleday who work behind the scenes day in and day out without recognition.

In particular I want to thank Carolyn Curtis for helping me get this book on paper. Without her help and her prose this project would not have been possible. I also want to thank a dear friend, Angela Hunt. She coauthored my first book and helped my literary career blossom.

Finally, I want to thank my family members for their prayers throughout my life. Their prayers have sustained me and protected me all the days of my life. I also want to thank my husband, John, for his support and encouragement. He knows the real Heather, and the real miracle is he still loves me.

BELIEVING THE PROMISE

1.

TODAY'S SCRIPTURE:
But seek ye first the kingdom of God, and his righteousness; and all these things shall be added unto you. (Matthew 6:33, KJV)

In my travels and public-speaking engagements, people often ask me questions that seem to have the same theme: How should I get started? How does a young woman initiate the series of events that leads to a goal such as the Miss America title? How does a bride begin her married life? How does anyone begin his day?

My answer can be summed up in this verse, Matthew 6:33, "But seek ye first the kingdom of God, and his righteousness; and all these things shall be added unto you." My reliance on the wisdom of this verse as "the way to start" is true whether I am responding as Miss America 1995, the wife of John McCallum or a young woman just stumbling out of bed. I believe my first act, my first goal—my first *instinct*—must be to seek God, His kingdom and His righteousness.

My *first* thought when awakening, my *first* activity as I begin my day, my *first* priority when I begin a life step as important and complex as marriage is to focus on God, to put Him *first*. Not *my* goal but His; not *my* will but His.

By seeking God first, I was motivated to aspire to the Miss America title as a platform for demonstrating how He has guided and blessed my life. Me, a deaf woman. Me, a girl who grew up seeing people laugh at jokes I could not hear, share intimacies I could not quite understand, discuss plans I had to work extra hard to fit into. Me, a child who knew rejection and misunderstanding at school. Me, a daughter of divorce. Me, an aspiring dancer who learned to depend on my heart to "hear" music that others heard with their ears.

As a bride I entered marriage with the conviction that both John and I must seek God first before each other. The triangular relationship that is often depicted graphically, with God at the top of the triangle and the husband and wife in the bottom two corners, means that each of us—John and myself—must seek God *individually*. We must know His will for each of us as a person, and then we can relate to each other as a married couple. Only then are we prepared to do so.

My first thought when I awaken is: *What is God's will for me today?* This seeking Him first—before thinking about my to-do list, before planning what I'll wear, before even throwing back the covers—this process focuses my attention and my heart. It sets a tone of obedience for the rest of day.

I will tell you more about my understanding of the word "seek" and also what I believe to be the promise Jesus makes at the end of this one key verse, but first I must give you some background.

AM I A BIBLE SCHOLAR?

I'm not a biblical scholar nor a theologian. I'm a seeker like you. Every day I add a little more to my understanding of God and His plan for my life. I do this through a deliberate process called seeking.

For me, seeking involves regular prayer; daily Bible study; interaction with other believers at my church and the larger faith community; disciplines such as fasting and tithing; and obedience ranging from my public profession of faith to a lifestyle of service. Although I am a seeker, I sin and require daily forgiveness. I fall short of God's will for my life. I disappoint myself and Him too, I'm sure. So this book of meditations comes entirely from my own life experiences, not from academic knowledge.

You'll find I use a favorite Scripture with each devotional. My comments on each verse are based on my personal perspective. I rely on anecdotes—some from my time in the public eye, others from my private life.

Yet, although I cannot claim biblical scholarship, I

make a deep commitment to you as a reader. I promise to be real. I promise to be myself.

My life hasn't always been easy. There were failures on my way to the success of winning the Miss America title. I experienced some pain during the year of my reign, which I will reveal—as well as the happiness, of course. Growing up deaf was tough; that presented its own complications and insecurities. Although I married a wonderful, handsome man, my dating life before John came along had some struggles and doubts. And, as I write this, I'm a college student trying to juggle homework with marriage and with more demands for public appearances than I can accept.

WHICH BRINGS UP THE REASON . . .

I decided to write a book of meditations. My faith is one of the characteristics people seem to know about me—I pray that anyone who knows the name Heather Whitestone Mc-Callum will think of me first and foremost as a Christian (although I must admit that "the deaf Miss America" probably comes to mind too). I'm known to be honest, even outspoken, about my journey with God. Interviewers, audiences, even people on the street have asked, "Heather, what Scriptures are meaningful to you and why?"

And so I decided that a book of devotions must come from my heart. The verses I use, the comments I write, even the words of prayer I suggest you pray—they all must reflect my passion for truly *seeking God first,* for beginning the

4

day with Him, for searching for His will in all of life's decisions, for discovering Him in quiet moments as well as dramatic bolts of lightning and claps of thunder.

I believe that a walk with God is dynamic. It's a thrilling journey. It's also a pensive search inside oneself. And so, just as I have committed to sharing intimate stories from my life, I promise not to hold back in telling you what the Bible means to me.

I will tell you when a passage has jolted me out of the blue. I will share what has touched me to the core of my being. I will confront you with realities—based on God's Word—which are meaningful to me; of course, it's entirely your choice whether to accept them as your own truths.

For example, this passage from Matthew tells us to seek God *first.* I take that literally. For me, it means sitting down with my Bible and a prayer list first thing in the morning. For me, it means consulting God's Word and talking to Him about an important life decision before consulting friends and family, before researching the subject and certainly before making a rash decision based on emotion. For me, it means seeking His will even when I am not in a crisis; that is, cultivating such an intimate, daily walk with the Lord that I literally know Him and can almost anticipate what He will say to me when I call on Him in times of great need or stress.

HOW TO USE THIS BOOK

Be comforted—all the meditations beyond this one are much, much shorter! In fact, most are one to two pages in length. I expect each will take three to five minutes—tops!

Of course, you're welcome to spend more time, because that's the point. Hopefully, you are developing a relationship with God whether you're using my book or another resource. And, like any other relationship, it takes time, time spent together, *quality* time spent together.

I'll give you an analogy. Let's say you meet someone you want to get to know better. Almost immediately the two of you whip out your calendars and begin comparing times to do something together—"How about coffee on Thursday, or lunch next week?" You make a commitment right then and there. You know that a relationship takes time, that commodity we're all short of but which we have to invest when the relationship warrants it.

And who is more important to spend time with than God?

I find that time with God—reading His Word, meditating and praying—needs to be a part of my *daily* routine or, frankly, I'm out of sorts, my life is out of whack. Can you relate to this?

So I've compiled ninety-nine meditations that consist of a Scripture, my comments and a recommended prayer. I use several versions of the Bible, not only to share with you the wording that I found helpful but also to celebrate the richness of scriptural language.

For example, "Seek ye first . . ." may sound a bit old-fashioned. And it should! It was taken from the King James Version. Yet I love this wording, because it is so traditional in the best sense—it's something we can depend on, just like the message behind the wording.

In this book's next meditation I chose a more modern version, the New International, to put into the most straightforward language I could find the advice Jesus was giving that led up to the famous "Seek ye first . . ." verse.

What I hope you will do is use this book daily. I suggest that you commit to a regular time and a regular place, and make this a must-do part of your routine.

Do you know how some people would never dream of a day without some activity that is important to them? I know a man who finds time every day to read the sports page. He's a hard worker, and he feels he owes it to himself to spend that time on something he really enjoys. It's a rare day when he doesn't take fifteen minutes to curl up behind the sports page and devour it. I know a woman who wouldn't go to bed with her makeup still on her face if her life depended on it. Her mother told her years ago that it would dry out her face, and so she committed to always cleaning her face before she goes to bed no matter how tired she is. Neither of these is a life-or-death activity. They're just part of the daily routines of these people. They no longer think about doing these things, no longer make a decision about whether or not to carry through with them. They just do it, as the Nike commercial says.

And so I think it should be with daily meditations.

THE LIFESTYLE OF SEEKING GOD FIRST

I hope you choose to take this walk with me by reading Scriptures I've come to love and my thoughts about each based on my own life. And then maybe you will pray the words I've included at the end of each devotional. Each prayer is meant to reinforce the "lesson" I share from my experiences. Perhaps you will add words of your own.

However, my real prayer is that these ninety-nine meditations will encourage you to pursue a *lifestyle* of seeking God first. That is, you will not only come to know the Lord more intimately, you will learn to depend on Him daily—for wisdom, guidance, protection, discipline and love.

Reread the second half of the verse: ". . . and all these things shall be added unto you." I have three comments.

First, this verse says God promises to provide for us. And I know His promise is true. I have experienced it over and over again in my own life. I encourage you to believe it and seek Him too. The rewards are immeasurable.

Second, God is not a genie in a bottle. He provides all our needs, including things as mundane as our clothing (you'll read more about this in the next meditation). But reading His Word, meditating on it and then praying is not some magic formula that results in His being good to you. He does that because He's God!

Third, the reason to seek Him *first*, before any other goal or activity of your day or your life, is not just practical (you would do your workout before you take a shower—right?—not in the reverse order). It's also a way to prioritize your entire life. It's a new and healthy habit to form. It's a lifestyle you can cultivate.

Our next meditation will put "Seek ye first . . ." into context. If you are not familiar with this wonderful passage, you may be surprised to find what Jesus was talking about when he said: "Seek ye first . . ."

PRAYER:
God, I am seeking You now, right this minute, today. I believe Your promise. Amen.

2.

Therefore I tell you, do not worry about your life, what you will eat or drink; or about your body, what you will wear. Is not life more important than food, and the body more important than clothes? Look at the birds of the air; they do not sow or reap or store away in barns, and yet your Heavenly Father feeds them. Are you not much more valuable than they? Who of you by worrying can add a single hour to his life? And why do you worry about clothes? See how the lilies of the field grow. They do not labor or spin. Yet I tell you that not even Solomon in all his splendor was dressed like one of these. If that is how God clothes the grass of the field, which is here today and tomorrow is thrown into the fire, will he not much more clothe you, O you of little faith? So do not worry, saying, "What shall we eat?" or "What shall we drink?" or "What shall we wear?" For the pagans run after all these things, and your Heavenly Father knows that you need them. But seek first his kingdom and his righteousness, and all these things will be given to you as well. Therefore do not worry about tomorrow, for tomorrow will worry about itself. Each day has enough trouble of its own. (Matthew 6:25–34, NIV)

I promised that most meditations will be short, and this is one.

The beautiful words above speak for themselves. There's little I can add other than encouragement to believe them and take them to heart.

For no matter what our experience has been with an earthly Father, our dependence on the Heavenly Father can be total and complete. He will care for us, and no amount of worry on our part will help. In fact, it may hinder: Worry may distract us from "seeking Him first."

Ask yourself this: Has worry ever added *anything* to your life? I would be very surprised if you said yes. Of course, attention to detail—watching out for what's important to your teacher or your boss or your family—that's important and a legitimate concern.

But how often do you worry about whether your clothes are right? Whether a friend really cares about you? Whether your family understands you?

As we grow older, we must learn to distinguish between *worry* and *concern*. Concern can be necessary at times. But worry is a spiritually immature approach to life, and can be, frankly, self-indulgent.

Worry itself, that emotion which can tie us into knots, is what this verse addresses. And I submit to you that worry does not help. Worry hinders. Worry can separate us from the love of God because it draws our attention to *our* agenda, not His.

And so I urge you to consider this lesson from God's Word. I urge you to accept that His words to us are this practical, this comforting, this relevant.

As you go deeper and deeper into Scripture, you will find that the lessons are not confined to the first century, the years right after Christ's life, death and resurrection. They apply to us today, people entering a new millennium, people seeking answers that apply to a confusing and complicated life. His words are timeless.

PRAYER:
Heavenly Father, I am so grateful for Your many provisions. You care for me more than Your other creatures and creation, the birds and the grasses, and yet, as a human being, I am prone to worry. Remind me throughout the day that You will provide. I seek You now, as I set about my tasks. Amen.

3.

For nothing is impossible with God. (Luke 1:37, NIV)

As you know, being Miss America is about more than beauty and personality and talent. The pageant rewards women who have the depth of character to be a role model for others. Often character is expressed in "platforms," much as a political candidate expresses a platform—or an agenda, a theme, a series of values that can motivate people to reach their full potential.

My Miss America platform emphasized five points. They were known as the STARS program, because a star has five points. I gave a great deal of thought to the five points of my program, because I knew that for many years to come, girls who were coming to terms with their young womanhood during the year of my reign as Miss America would be influenced by the ideals behind the five points of STARS.

In other words, I knew that STARS had to be substantial, not just a clever idea that the judges of the Miss America contest could latch on to and use to justify their choice for the winner, which for the year 1995 happened to be me. The five points of STARS had to resonate with young women wherever I traveled and spoke, and they had to stand the test of time. They had to be advice that I myself had taken. They had to be advice that I knew from personal experience would work. They had to be advice that I thought would inspire.

And so these are the five points I spoke of wherever I made a personal appearance or had an opportunity to speak to someone one-on-one: develop a positive attitude, believe in your dreams, work hard, face your weaknesses and obstacles, and build a dependable support team.

Some days during that year of constant travel, I had to listen to my own advice. The experience was both exhilarating and draining. Often, I was surrounded by people, yet I was lonely. In many ways, the year of my reign as Miss America was a microcosm of my life as a deaf person: silence inside of chaos. The walk down the runway in Atlantic City for any young woman winning that title marks the beginning of a very, very long journey. It's one well worth taking, of course, but nevertheless exhausting. I write this with total respect for the pageant, its organizers and participants, but—if I am to share my heart with readers of this book of devotionals—I must be truly honest. It is a wonderful but at the same time stressful year. It caused me to look inside myself and to question a lot of who I was and what I was representing.

And so I came up with a second five-point program, one that springs directly from God's Word and which sustained me through an almost overwhelming twelve months of responsibilities. I'm so proud to present this second program to you! It's called TDPFL, using the first letter of each point: take time to be quiet, don't forget to dream, populate your life with positive people, forgive the hurt and anger of the past, love yourself as God loves you.

I believe these points, TDPFL, more closely resemble the path God wants us to take. Figuring them out was like hearing God translate the STARS program into His own sweet language, the promise of Luke 1:37, a verse that I wrote in my journal several years before I began my pursuit of the Miss America title. I am bolder now in telling people that my inspiration must come directly from God's Word.

I expect that as I grow older and wiser, I will continue to refine the five points of my star to reflect my walk with Him. In the meantime, I hope and pray that the TDPFL points will help as you set out to make meditating on Scripture and prayer a priority in your daily activity.

PRAYER:

Dear Lord, I take time now to be quiet. I am dreaming with You. Please populate my life with positive people. I forgive the hurt and anger of the past. Teach me to love myself as You love me. Amen.

4.

Meanwhile, the people were waiting for Zechariah and wondering why he stayed so long in the temple. When he came out, he could not speak to them. They realized he had seen a vision in the temple, for he kept making signs to them but remained unable to speak. (Luke 1:21–22, NIV)

Let's expand on the five-point program I wrote about in yesterday's meditation. It's called TDPFL, using the first letter of each point. The first point is: Take time to be quiet.

Frankly, as a deaf woman, I live in almost total silence. I know the benefits of being in a quiet, reflective mode. Sometimes I can block out the world, and that can be good when I need to focus and concentrate. But I don't wish my type of silence on you, although I'm sure God meant for me to be deaf and so I don't resent it.

What I encourage you to do is *to go to the Lord* in silence. By this I mean go to Him in prayer but without re-

17

quests, without a list of complaints and problems, without an agenda.

Go to Him in a spirit of submission, giving yourself to Him as you are, not as you wish to become. This kind of truthfulness is cleansing.

Go to Him with an attitude of expectation, knowing that He does speak to His children, not audibly, perhaps, but in our hearts.

I find that sometimes I need just to *listen* to God, to turn off my mind and enjoy being in His presence. Being quiet with God is refreshing and often instructive. It invites clarity. It energizes me and prepares me for whatever is ahead.

Please take a moment to reread the passage from Luke at the beginning of this meditation. Zechariah, a priest, has just been told by an angel of the Lord that he will become a father for the first time, a miraculous circumstance since he and his wife, Elizabeth, are getting along in years. The baby will be known to the world as John the Baptist, the one who prepares the way for Jesus when both men are adults. But at the time he is told this remarkable message, Zechariah questions it and expresses his disbelief. The angel then tells him that he will immediately be struck silent and will speak again "at the proper time."

Well, sure enough, Zechariah is unable to speak throughout his wife's pregnancy. Then, after Elizabeth gives birth and Zechariah confirms by using a writing tablet that the baby's name is to be John, he suddenly is able to speak again. And what words he uses! He says to his baby son, John: "And you, my child, will be called a prophet of the Most High; for you will go on before the Lord to prepare the way for him, to give his people the knowledge of salvation through the forgiveness of their sins, because of the tender mercy of our God, by which the rising sun will come to us from heaven to shine on those living in darkness and in the shadow of death, to guide our feet into the path of peace." (Luke 1:76–79, NIV)

Have you ever heard such a succinct and yet beautiful explanation of the Gospel? Zechariah, who had not spoken for nine months, was brimming with words, such special words! Zechariah's quiet time, plus his anointing by the Holy Spirit, prepared him for such a prophecy.

What will the Lord reveal to you if you give Him your attention in silence?

PRAYER:

Lord, too often I come to You with a list of requests, things I need, things I want, things I want You to "fix," as though You are my earthly father. Today, I come to You humbly and quietly, willing to hear You, willing just to be present with You whether I actually "hear" You or not. Please accept my silence as eagerness to know You more fully. Amen.

5.

And it shall come to pass in the last days, saith God, I will pour out of my Spirit upon all flesh: and your sons and your daughters shall prophesy, and your young men shall see visions, and your old men shall dream dreams. (Acts 2:16, KJV)

The second point of my star, TDPFL, is: Don't forget to dream.

Naturally, I'm not talking about snoozing in school or on the job or any other time when you should be staying awake!

No, that's not the kind of dreaming I mean, although I know that literal dreams, which are natural and therefore made by God, are part of His plan for our restful sleep. (Consider, for example, how many people in the Bible learned something useful in their dreams. Mary and Joseph were warned to flee to Egypt, and then God used another dream to tell them when it was safe to return to Israel. The

Old Testament character of Joseph even made a career of interpreting dreams.)

What I mean by remembering to dream is this: Allow your mind to wander a bit, to explore options that at first you might not consider, to be creative by stretching yourself beyond limitations you may have imposed on yourself.

I believe that much of what we discover in our hearts has been placed there by the Holy Spirit. This verse describes the outpouring of the Spirit, which includes the amazing phenomenon of dreaming.

And the kind of dreaming I'm talking about, that step just beyond making short-term plans, should be built into our "mental" schedule. We should allow our minds to wander into unexplored territory, to think of ideas never before tried, to go where we've never dared. Who knows where that thought process may lead if we turn it loose?

Consider the kind of dream that Dr. Martin Luther King spoke of in his famous speech delivered in Washington, D.C.—"I have a dream . . ." Certainly, the great Dr. King did not literally mean he laid down to sleep one night and had this dream of equality for all people, no matter what the color of their skin. I believe what he was describing was a great idea, a wonderful vision, a thought so powerful that he shared it with one of the largest crowds ever gathered in one place in America. And, in so sharing his dream, he inspired an entire nation.

If we're too focused on the here and now, on our everyday circumstances, we may miss an opportunity for something great to happen. In other words, we need to allow ideas that may be placed in our hearts by the Spirit of God to bubble up to the surface, where we can explore them.

Many great people have accomplished remarkable things because they dared to dream. They allowed their nugget of an idea to blossom and flourish until it became a plan. Think of Christopher Columbus. Think of Clara Barton. Think of Booker T. Washington. Think of Henry Ford. Think of Bill Gates. Columbus is credited with discovering America. Barton, a teacher and nurse, founded the American Red Cross. Washington, an educator and social reformer, founded Tuskegee Institute. Ford revolutionized American industry with his vision for mass production. And Gates, founder of Microsoft, has affected the global marketplace.

I'm in no position to judge whether the ideas that originated in these people's hearts were placed there directly by God, but we can see what resulted from these people dreaming and then following those dreams.

What's in your heart just below the surface? It may be a dream placed there by God.

PRAYER:

I thank You, God, for giving me not only the encouragement but the freedom to follow my dreams. Please help me
to discern which are foolhardy and which are wise. And
then give me the strength to follow them. Amen.

6.

Then Mary took about a pint of pure nard, an expensive perfume; she poured it on Jesus' feet and wiped his feet with her hair. And the house was filled with the fragrance of the perfume. But one of his disciples, Judas Iscariot, who was later to betray him, objected, "Why wasn't this perfume sold and the money given to the poor? It was worth a year's wages." He did not say this because he cared about the poor but because he was a thief; as keeper of the money bag, he used to help himself to what was put into it. "Leave her alone," Jesus replied. "It was intended that she should save this perfume for the day of my burial. You will always have the poor among you, but you will not always have me." (John 12:3–7, NIV)

The third point of my five-point star: Populate your life with positive people.

I have selected this touching scene from the last week in Jesus' life to illustrate my point that the wrong people can drag you down, whereas good people can bring you joy.

24

In this passage, Judas, who is a thief, ridicules an extravagant and loving act done by Mary, a friend to Jesus and the twelve disciples. But Jesus recognizes her act of generosity and knows that she has her priorities in order. He instructs Judas, "Leave her alone."

Don't we sometimes wish Jesus were here to tell the people who hurt us to "leave her alone"? That is a wonderful fantasy, but actually, we do have a solution that is almost as satisfying. He has provided us with the wisdom and discernment to recognize positive people. Those are the ones who can lift our spirits, who can encourage us with helpful feedback, who can challenge us to do better.

I know of a wonderful ministry called Heart to Heart that is based on women mentoring other women. It works like this: Women are paired with a woman at least ten years younger. The two women become prayer partners, they study the Bible together, and they hold each other accountable for goals they set. The older woman is viewed as the wiser, although both understand and accept that they can learn from the other, no matter what her age. They also have a great deal of fun. Some of the pairs spend Saturdays shopping or helping each other with cooking and crafts. Each "pairing" is meant to last only nine months so that neither feels burdened by an open-ended relationship. Of course, many of the pairs remain friends after the nine months has ended.

The beauty of this kind of ministry is that a participant develops the habit of being in a relationship with a woman who is a positive influence on her.

Men develop partnerships like this too. The Promise Keepers program encourages men to become involved in accountability relationships with other men. I know guys who meet over coffee one morning each week for prayer and Bible study. They grow close in such a setting, making themselves vulnerable to the other guys in the group. They admit their failures, share their dreams, talk about their needs. They model good behavior and provide a positive influence for one another. And, after experiencing such positive relationships, negative ones seem unfulfilling by comparison. The participants are hungry for more that are this satisfying.

Who populates your life? Do you hang out with people who lift you up or bring you down? What kind of people do you think God wants you to spend time with?

PRAYER:

Dear God, I realize that I've been a little sloppy about my relationships. I need to be better about selecting the people I spend time with, the people who influence me, the people with whom I share my time on earth. Help me to be more discerning about finding people who are positive, people who know You and can help me to know You better. And then make me a friend to them in return. Amen.

7.

Get rid of all bitterness, passion, and anger. No more shouting or insults! No more hateful feeling of any sort! Instead, be kind and tender-hearted to one another, and forgive one another, as God has forgiven you in Christ. (Ephesians 4:31–32, Good News for Modern Man)

The fourth point of my five-point star named TDPFL is: Forgive the hurt and anger of the past.

I wish I could say this is easy for me. It is not. I have experienced deep hurts (and I've probably hurt several people myself), and forgiveness is hard to do.

The only way I can accomplish this is through Christ. The forgiveness I experience through His death and resurrection is humanly impossible to understand and fully appreciate. Therefore, all I can do is know about it, believe it and claim it for myself. I do those three things as a conscious act. And so it is with forgiveness. I consciously have

27

to forgive people who have hurt me, whether I *feel* like it or not.

In other words, forgiveness is not a feeling; it is an *action.* It is a step I take. Whether or not it happens should not be a direct result of my feelings. If that were the case, I probably would never forgive anybody, because I rarely feel like doing it.

Forgiving the hurt and anger of the past is something I just *have* to accomplish from time to time—like cleaning out a drawer or paying the bills. It's a task that *has* to be done. If I don't, my sock drawer becomes such a mess that I can't find a matching pair or my bills pile up on the kitchen counter and become overwhelming.

Hurt and anger can become like piles of unmatched socks or unpaid bills: They accumulate. Or they seem scarier than they are. They distract us by their undeserved importance. And all this misery just because we haven't taken care of them!

I believe that forgiveness occurs in my heart. Oh, it's nice to be able to say to my friend, "I forgive you. The past is the past, and it's behind me now." But sometimes saying those words directly to her is a bad idea. Sometimes that brings up a subject which is best left buried.

And yet we cannot bury the pain in our heart. That's called denial, and it's dangerous to our health—including our spiritual health. Because when we harbor something bad in our heart, then we are separated from God. We are not

28

experiencing the forgiveness He has modeled for us with the death of His son for our sins. When we deliberately cling to hurt and pain, refusing to forgive, we are acting as though we "don't get it"—don't comprehend what God was doing by allowing His son to die in our place.

So this for me is the most compelling reason to forgive—it's to be Godlike in my actions. Are you willing to do for others what God has so generously done for you?

PRAYER:

As I ask You for forgiveness for myself, Lord, I also ask for the compassion and generosity of heart to forgive those who have hurt me. Thank You for forgiving me for my sins. Now I ask for the ability to forgive others for hurts that are not nearly as grievous as the ones I have committed against You. Amen.

8.

TODAY'S SCRIPTURE:

. . . Love your neighbor as much as you love yourself. (Matthew 22:39, The Living Bible)

The fifth and final point of my five-point program begins with *L*: Love yourself as God loves you.

I will illustrate this point by admitting how difficult it has been for me to learn how to do this properly. In fact, I will admit that I am still working on it and probably will for the rest of my life.

You see, it takes a certain amount of self-confidence to "run" for something. My husband has run for public office in Georgia. I was in the running for several pageants, including Miss Alabama and Miss America. But I often consider whether self-confidence is a God-given trait or something we have created for ourselves.

When this question really begins to worry me, I read these words of Jesus. In this famous passage, He answers a question posed to him: "Teacher, which is the greatest commandment in the Law?" (verse 36) In the next verse, Jesus replies: "Love the Lord your God with all your heart and with all your soul and with all your mind." Then he goes on to say: "And the second is like it: 'Love your neighbor as yourself.' "

I'm convinced that many people are conceited, way too big on themselves, and I pray I'm not like that. But I understand this teaching to mean that, if we are to *effectively* love our neighbor, then we must first love ourselves.

This implies self-respect (though not self-absorption). It also implies a good understanding of ourselves (as children of God, which, by definition, makes us special). And this implies the ability to love ourselves (although certainly not worship ourselves, an act which should be reserved for our attitude toward God).

I'm fascinated to think that Jesus would state that the second commandment is "like the first." It invites us to celebrate who we are as God's children, as God's own—in other words, as having worth because of Who created us, not because of any value we have created for ourselves.

Of course, I think God wants us to enjoy our successes, the titles we may have captured, the pinnacles we may have climbed. But I'm convinced that He urges us to examine this matter of loving ourselves. I consider it my responsibility to find the "edges" of this act of self-love—to learn to do it properly in the first place and then to discern when I have gone too far.

PRAYER:

Jesus, I want to apply Your teachings, including learning to first love myself, so that I may, in turn, love my neighbor. Guide me in this learning process so that I go as far as will honor You, but not too far. It is my desire to love myself in the perfect way that You love me—without conceit or self-absorption. And as I grow in healthy self-respect, I pray that I will become more and more like You. Amen.

9.

TODAY'S SCRIPTURE:
. . . do not lose heart when he rebukes you, because the Lord disciplines those he loves, and he punishes everyone he accepts as a son. (Hebrews 12:5–6, NIV)

In the last meditation I spoke of developing godly self-respect. As a follow-up, I can think of no better Scripture than this one to meditate on today.

It was a great revelation to me to realize that, when God allows me to go through adversity, He is strengthening me. And the reason He is strengthening me is because I am His child. He wants me to "grow up" to be strong, to feel secure in His love for me, to become mature in my understanding of Him. He is my parent, my *perfect* parent.

God has certainly allowed failure in my life—as well as victory. The road to Atlantic City was rocky and rough. I experienced big disappointments at several pageants on my way to being crowned Miss America in 1995. For example, it took me three attempts to win the Miss Alabama contest.

Now, I'm not saying that losing those first contests are specific examples of the Lord disciplining me—that explanation would be too simplistic. But I know that He *allowed* those losses—and, ultimately, the lessons they taught me.

I am incredibly grateful for that perfect parenting, because the truth is, I wasn't mature enough in the earlier pageants to handle the responsibility of representing my state.

And, yes, I admit to you there have been times when I know the Lord has actually punished me. Those times were hard to endure, but now I understand not only why I was being punished but what was the greater meaning: because I am His child.

He loves me as a *perfect* parent loves a son or daughter. Have you considered this truth in your own relationship with Him?

PRAYER:
Heavenly Father, thank You for loving me enough to discipline me, for rebuking me when I go wrong, for accepting me as Your child. Amen.

10.

Let them praise his name with dancing. (Psalm 149:3, NIV)

Near the end of the Book of Psalms is this delightful verse. It invited me to dance exuberantly for God, as a form of worship, as a way to demonstrate my love for Him and to show it to others in a public, yet intimate, way.

On the final night of the Miss America pageant, my ballet performance was accompanied by Sandi Patti's song, "Via Dolorosa." Although I had practiced my dance hundreds of times, I will never forget what happened on that particular night.

This may sound weird, but it felt to me as if I had no control over my body. I had been dancing ballet for sixteen years by the time I performed for the pageant judges and the audience, and I knew my body well. But that night, I am certain I was not dancing alone. It was as though one of God's angels was behind me, guiding me, helping to straighten my shoulders and balance me as I was on my toes. It was one of the times in my life when God revealed Himself to me directly.

Thus, I believe it was a truly inspired performance—a time when both my movements as a dancer and the music, which others could hear, inspired people to experience God's love.

Are there times when God makes you aware of Him? What talent, skill or interest has He given you? Give serious thought to the source of what draws your attention. Give thanks if you believe it is *the* Source.

PRAYER:
I come to you, dear Lord, with whatever talent, ability or skill You have given me, and I use it to praise Your name. Amen.

11.

You turned my wailing into dancing; you removed my sackcloth and clothed me with joy, that my heart may sing to you and not be silent, O Lord my God, I will give you thanks forever. (Psalm 30:11–12, NIV)

One of the most common questions I am asked is "Heather, how do you hear the music?"

Well, of course, I don't actually hear it, at least not perfectly. I do wear a hearing aid, which allows me to pick up a tiny bit of sound. But, for dancing, I rely on God to lead me. So dancing has become a great discipline for my life of reliance on Him.

In my autobiography, *Listening with My Heart* (Doubleday, 1997), I tell how I experience what I call "silent music." Silent music, in its most basic terms, is the residue of music I pick up in my hearing aid, which is then amplified by my imagination.

Just as I "hear" God's voice in my heart (and so do you,

I hope and pray!), I "hear" the music. And within my heart is the desire to leap and twirl and float in the air—all as a form of worship. Of course, there's no denying that dancing is fun too! It's great exercise. It's an art form. It's relaxation. It's self-expression.

During my childhood, it was a route to escape. When I was at school, I couldn't understand what the students were saying. I could see their lips moving (and, to some extent, I could keep up with their conversations by reading their lips). But it wasn't the same. I felt isolated. So when I joined a dance group, I was relieved to learn that no one communicated with their voices, only their bodies. I understood them and felt a sense of belonging. I rejoiced.

When my parents were going through the struggles that led to their divorce, I could retreat to my room and lose myself in ballet. I could be alone in the house and dance my troubles away. I even became involved in dancing with other deaf people and was almost able to forget I had a disability.

In fact, although I accept my label as the first Miss America with a disability, I consider the interaction between myself and God while I dance to be a very special *ability*.

I urge you to find the special abilities God has given to you and that you use them to praise Him.

Please take a moment now to reflect on what talents, skills and interests He has given you. And then consider how you are using them. Is there any room for improvement? Could you practice more? Could you work out more? Could you study more?

You may be a student or a young mother or a career person just starting out. You might have an interest in playing the piano or running marathons or studying a language. Maybe these can be done for God's glory. Can they?

PRAYER:
Show me, Lord, how to praise You with my special abilities given to me by You. Open my eyes to the possibilities. I give You thanks forever. Amen.

12.

TODAY'S SCRIPTURE:
But the pot he was shaping from the clay was marred in his hands; so the potter formed it into another pot, shaping it as seemed best to him. (Jeremiah 18:4, NIV)

Doctors are not sure what the illness was that caused me to lose my hearing.

I was only eighteen months old when my parents rushed me to the hospital. I had begun that day with a slight fever—what appeared to be the start of a typical childhood ailment. My parents had nursed my sisters, Stacey and Melissa, through several illnesses—you know, chicken pox, that sort of thing. All families go through this. It's part of childhood. Now my parents figured it was my turn as the baby of the family.

But this fever turned bad. It soared above 104 degrees and turned into a real life-or-death situation, a parent's worst nightmare.

Doctors administered two antibiotics. The medications

were strong but risky. Side effects included the possibility of blindness, deafness or mental retardation. Imagine my parents having to make such a decision. I ache for them when I think about it. Here was their youngest daughter, so small and fragile. Yet they went by the doctors' recommendation. It must have been a frightening time, but I feel they made the right choice.

The antibiotics did work, and my fever subsided. It was a long, uphill battle. I spent two weeks in the hospital and finally came home. However, my recovery was not complete. The massive infection I'd suffered left my body extremely weak.

Once, when I was being interviewed by Barbara Walters many years later, she ran footage of a home movie filmed right after I had returned from the hospital. It was my first time to ever see this clip, and, right there during the interview, my eyes welled up with tears. In the video I was flopping around like a pathetic rag doll, unable to run and play with my sisters, dependent on relatives even to sit up.

A few months later, my parents were to learn the awful truth: The illness and necessary treatment had left me profoundly deaf. Doctors predicted that I would not develop much verbal speech. They added that I probably would not progress beyond a third-grade education and recommended that I be enrolled in some sort of vocational training when I became an adult.

In other words, the doctors believed I would be far

more limited than I am today, thanks to the Potter's loving hands on me!

Has anyone ever expected less of you than what your Heavenly Father created with His own hands? Have *you* ever expected less of yourself? Perhaps you have more potential than you are demonstrating by the friends you have chosen, the way you spend your time, the priorities you set.

Please examine what the perfect Potter had in mind for you before you pray this prayer.

PRAYER:

Thanks to Your hands upon me, Lord, I am made exactly as You want me. Give me the grace to live with whatever opportunities and limitations You have given me. Amen.

13.

TODAY'S SCRIPTURE:
Blessed is the man who trusts in the Lord and has made the Lord his hope and confidence. He is like a tree planted along a riverbank, with its roots reaching deep into the water—a tree not bothered by the heat nor worried by long months of drought. Its leaves stay green and it goes right on producing all its luscious fruit. (Jeremiah 17:7–8, The Living Bible)

Now that I am married and hope someday to be a mother, I can almost imagine the terror that must have run through my mother's heart when she realized I was deaf.

It happened like this. The day was December 25, 1974, three months after my return from the hospital, where I had a rough recovery from a mysterious infection. Naturally, since it was Christmas Day, the house was decorated, and it was full of happy relatives sharing the joy of the season. No one was prepared for what they would learn about me as the day wore on.

My mother was working in the kitchen to get the traditional holiday dinner on the table. I can picture her bustling around chopping this and that, fixing what would be a feast. As she went about her routine, she opened a cabinet and, suddenly, onto the floor spilled a stack of pots and pans. They made a huge clatter, and everyone in the living room was startled by the loud noise.

Everyone, that is, but me. I continued to gaze at the lights on the Christmas tree. It was as though I were transfixed. The pretty colors were holding my toddler's attention. And the noise from the kitchen didn't faze me a bit.

My grandmother and aunt called my mother into the living room and told her what they had observed. Naturally, I was equally oblivious to the alarm in their voices. My mother brought a pan and wooden spoon and began banging them together directly behind me. But I had no idea she was even in the room with me. I heard nothing.

Although this was the beginning of a heart-wrenching discovery about their daughter, my parents eventually learned to make the best of things by providing me with a fine education (some of it among other deaf kids, which helped me learn to communicate better) and by supporting my pursuits such as ballet.

Let me assure you that deafness itself is not a reason to be unhappy. I had joy and dreams in my heart that, as I matured, I learned were placed there by God, whom I eventually grew to know in a personal way. I firmly believe that the most handicapped people are those who are troubled by negative thoughts and low expectations.

If He is not your root, your source of a firm foundation, then I urge you to take that step by joining me in the prayer at the end of this meditation.

PRAYER:

God, I trust You to keep me upright as a tree with a deep and well-nourished root. Thank You for providing me with green leaves. I pray that You will help me to produce good fruit. Amen.

14.

TODAY'S SCRIPTURE:
My lover spoke and said to me, "Arise, my darling, my beautiful one, and come with me . . ." (Song of Solomon 2:10, NIV)

My marriage to John McCallum is the source of much of the inspiration that I plan to share with you throughout these devotionals. But I will start with the story of his proposal—giving you some insight into our romance.

Women remember every detail of such a moment! And I will share them all with you. But first some background on how we met and fell in love.

I began dating John during my year as Miss America 1995. He worked in the office of the Speaker of the House of Representatives, Newt Gingrich, who represented John's home district in Georgia. During my travels as Miss America, I went to Washington, D.C., and so, naturally, the Speaker's office was one of my stops.

Maintaining a relationship during those months I was on the road was hectic, to say the least, but John and I managed to stay in touch. We knew something special was going on between us, and so we followed our hearts and eventually fell in love. I wouldn't recommend a long-distance relationship in general, but somehow it worked for us.

Finally, one night about two months after I surrendered my title, we were together again in Washington, D.C. We were about to go out to dinner, but he suggested we swing by Newt's office to pick up some "homework."

"I didn't know you had homework," I said, laughing.

I had a sneaky suspicion something was strange when he led me to the balcony of the Capitol building. We gazed toward the Washington Monument, a bright moon illuminating it dramatically. What a romantic setting!

But I was hungry.

"John, you lied to me," I said, teasing him about his lame excuse of picking up "homework," of all things. It wasn't like him to do this. I knew something was going on, but I couldn't put my finger on what it was.

Then he did something really strange, considering we had plans. He invited me to sit on a bench. This night was getting weirder by the minute! And I thought he was behaving very strangely, talking about nothing important while I was growing hungrier by the minute. Finally, I protested and said I was ready to leave.

But John wanted to stay on the balcony a few minutes longer. I noticed he seemed overwhelmed and nervous. Suddenly, he fell to one knee. His heart immediately spoke to

47

mine, although I watched him say the words and read his lips.

"Heather," he said, "I love you with all my heart, all my mind, and all my soul. I want to spend the rest of my life with you. Will you marry me?"

Of course, I answered an exuberant "Yes!"

He pulled a ring from his pocket and gently slid it onto my finger.

I was thrilled beyond words. And, guess what? I found that I was not the least bit hungry anymore!

PRAYER:

Thank You, Lord, for the blessing of loving relationships that You bring into our lives. Amen.

15.

TODAY'S SCRIPTURE:

Shadrach, Meshach and Abednego replied to the king, "O Nebuchad-nezzar, we do not need to defend ourselves before you in this matter. If we are thrown into the blazing furnace, the God we serve is able to save us from it, and he will rescue us from your hand, O king. But even if he does not, we want you to know, O king, that we will not serve your gods or worship the image of gold you have set up." (Daniel 3:16–18, NIV)

Three relatively obscure (but inspiring) men from the Book of Daniel made an impression on me that influenced my decision to dance to Christian music during the Miss America pageant.

Those men were Shadrach, Meshach and Abednego. They were Israelites who had been exiled against their will to Babylon, where they were picked to enter into the king's service. These three young men, according to Daniel 1:3, were "without any physical defect, handsome, showing aptitude for every kind of learning, well informed, quick to understand, and qualified to serve in the king's palace." They would be taught the language and literature of the Babylonians. In other words, they were the cream of the crop, and they would be given an opportunity to have a special place in the king's court.

But to do so meant accepting the gods and the faith of these pagan people. The three young men refused to do it even though it meant sacrificing their lives. Their choice was an act of great bravery and also loyalty to God.

The king was furious at their refusal to accept his offer and bend to his ways and customs. So he ordered the furnace to be heated up to seven times its normal temperature. As bellows forced air into the fire chamber, the furnace became so hot that some of the king's own soldiers died just by binding the three Israelites and getting close enough to toss them into the fire.

But the three men survived. The king looked inside and realized they were not burning. He called to them to come out. They stepped out, unharmed, to the gasps of the king and his advisers. Not a hair on their heads was singed. Their robes were not scorched. There was no smell of fire on them.

The king was so impressed by the protection of God on these three men that he said in Daniel 3:28–29: "Praise be to the God of Shadrach, Meshach and Abednego, who has sent his angel and rescued his servants! They trusted in him and defied the king's command and were willing to give up their lives rather than serve or worship any god except their own God. Therefore I decree that the people of any nation or language who say anything against the God of Shadrach, Meshach and Abednego be cut into pieces and their houses be turned into piles of rubble, for no other god can save in this way."

Here's why this story influenced me: If God could save these men from a fiery furnace, then surely He would bless my choice of Christian music in such a public display of my faith in Him. So against the advice of many, I selected Sandi Patti's song "Via Dolorosa." It was a time when I would be in the public eye, in a contest among the cream of the crop, and I could either take the "safe" road—no controversy but also no witness for the Lord—or I could take the "high" way and reveal for Whom I dance.

Obviously, I've never regretted taking that risk.

PRAYER:

Dear God, You are so faithful to reward us with victory over death and even salvation from humiliation when we take a public stand for You. Give me an opportunity today to show others how much I love and worship You. I promise You I will not let You down. Amen.

16.

TODAY'S SCRIPTURE:

Your beauty should not come from outward adornment, such as braided hair and the wearing of gold jewelry and fine clothes. Instead, it should be that of your inner self, the unfading beauty of a gentle and quiet spirit, which is of great worth in God's sight. (I Peter 3:3–4, NIV)

There is no denying the fact that a big element of the Miss America pageant is the beauty contest. Although my goal was to win a scholarship and to dance my ballet as a form of public worship to God, I also am pleased that my appearance won points from the judges. However, this aspect can be slightly awkward if people dwell on it to the exclusion of the other criteria for selection for the title.

If and when I become a mother, I hope to model healthy behavior to my children. That will include the routine of keeping myself physically fit and as neat and attractive as the years allow. I plan to grow old gracefully, knowing that wrinkles and gray hair eventually are inevitable; in fact, they are a part of God's plan. But I hope and pray that I don't put undue emphasis on this business of outward appearance. And that my children learn this lesson from me.

I'm firmly convinced that beauty from within—that which is of great worth in God's sight—is much more important and even valued by people who are honest with themselves. For, although it is entertaining to look at beautiful people, it is much more appealing to interact with those whose inner self draws you to them—through warmth, sincerity, interests beyond themselves, kindness, a spirit of goodness. That spirit (or Spirit) should be from God, who will fill us with a beauty that only He can provide.

That is the beauty which I now seek. And I know it will never fade with age.

PRAYER:
Bless me with an inner beauty, Lord, based on the assurance of Your love for me. Amen.

17.

TODAY'S SCRIPTURE:
. . . live a life of love, just as Christ loved us and gave himself up for us as a fragrant offering and sacrifice to God. (Ephesians 5:2, NIV)

As a participant in several "beauty" pageants before winning the Miss America title in 1995, I spent time backstage with many excited young women who, like me, primped and prepared themselves for scrutiny by judges. Sometimes we fixed each other's hair into elaborate arrangements on which a crown would sit firmly and proudly. We would help each other with glamorous makeup. And, of course, with all the perfumes used by the girls, the dressing area was a riot of fragrances. It was fun, but it also provided me with an object lesson on which to meditate.

This verse in Ephesians speaks of "fragrance," but it certainly doesn't mean Obsession by Calvin Klein! No, this New Testament Scripture refers to the fragrant offerings of sacrifices that were a "pleasing aroma" to the Lord as described in Old Testament passages such as Genesis 8:21; Exodus 29:18, 25, 41; and Leviticus 1:9, 13, 17. Take a few extra minutes today and familiarize yourself with these passages if you are surprised that the Bible speaks of fragrances. It is full of so many surprises!

In a practical sense, I see a connection between yesterday's lesson about inner beauty and the fragrant offering desired by God. Because Christians are to model our lives after Jesus, we need to fully understand how He "gave himself up"—that is, sacrificed not only His life but many of His pleasures.

And so, again, I see in this Scripture from Ephesians an admonishment not to put too much emphasis on the exterior. I'm not saying that I don't sometimes use delightful fragrances. I don't consider them evil; in fact, I think they are a blessing. But sometimes I see women wasting far too much time at the perfume counter making a selection for something that does not have the lasting value of Jesus' sacrifice for us on the cross. How we spend our time is a good indication of our priorities.

When I do become a mom, I hope to teach my children this value, which I firmly believe: What goes into our hearts is *far* more important than what goes on our bodies.

I trust that the Lord will provide me with creative object lessons and insights to convey this important concept.

In the meantime, I offer it to you now, if you have never thought of it.

PRAYER:
I am (literally!) eternally grateful, dear God, for the sacrifice of Your precious Son in exchange for my life. Amen.

18.

TODAY'S SCRIPTURE:

Even the Spirit of truth; whom the world cannot receive, because it seeth him not, neither knoweth him: but ye know him; for he dwelleth with you, and shall be in you. (John 14:17, KJV)

I heard about a loving afternoon of instruction between a man with technical skills—perhaps an engineer—and his five-year-old daughter. I'll call this man Jim and his daughter, Mandy. Try to picture them with me. Jim has a pocket protector (he's a proud nerd!), and little Mandy has dark curls and long eyelashes.

Well, with entry into school only a year away, Jim figured it was time to teach the youngster some computer fundamentals.

Patiently, Jim showed his daughter his computer. She had watched him use it many times, had even sat squirming in his lap a time or two as he banged out e-mails to friends and coworkers. But today was special, a time alone with her daddy with the focus on her, and so Mandy approached the machine with an attitude of wonder.

Like many in her generation, she wasn't intimidated by the maze of equipment with its many cables leading to the almond-colored components spread around Jim's basement workspace. And Mandy quickly grasped the basics: what happens when she touches the keyboard, why one instrument is called a "mouse," how images appear on a televisionlike screen.

Encouraged by her progress, Jim figured a lesson was in order on the importance of safety and computer security. With love, but also using a bit of what we adults might call techno-babble, he lectured about the various cords, why she needed to be careful around them, not only for her safety but to preserve work done on the computer.

Screwing her little face into a frown, Mandy appeared puzzled by the web of wires.

But her childlike reaction gave Jim an idea. He wanted his daughter to be comfortable with the computer, to like it, to *want* to use it as a learning tool.

So he launched into an analogy based on her rudimentary understanding of how a lamp works—that is, you twist a switch and a lightbulb begins to glow under a shade. The light is produced by something called electricity, which runs through a cable to an electric outlet in the wall. Mandy knew not to touch the outlet or to trip on the cord.

The object lesson ended when Jim told her that elec-

tricity was something she couldn't see but that it was powerful and resided inside an object she *could* see.

Suddenly, Mandy pointed to her heart and said with
authority: "Like where God lives!"

PRAYER:

Heavenly Father, I approach You with the simple faith of a
child, praising You for being the light that guides me in all
that I do. I know that sometimes I can "see" You and
sometimes I cannot, but You are no more or less real to me
at either time. I thank You for living in my heart, where it
counts. Amen.

19.

. . . God, the blessed and only Ruler, the King of kings and Lord of lords. (1 Timothy 6:15, NIV)

When I was a little girl I dreamed of being a princess. I suppose every girl entertains such a fantasy at some point in her childhood. Our parents read stories to us about princesses—they appear as characters in fairy tales and fables and nursery rhymes. Most of these were written at least a century ago.

In such innocent stories, the princess is beautiful, and she leads a life of ease, probably luxury. And, of course, her clothes are fabulous! If you are female, do you remember dressing a princess doll, perhaps combing her long, silky hair? You would dress her in flowing gowns, perhaps satin with an ermine collar, and place a crown on her lovely head—symbolic of her status as a royal.

In the modern world we still have princesses. I think of two—Grace of Monaco and Diana of England. Both were acclaimed for their beauty and accomplishments. Both died in tragic car accidents.

But wait! Before the memories of these two famous women evoke in your mind a sad replaying of their media-hounded lives, I want you to consider this: If you worship God, *you* are a princess! For what is a princess but the daughter of a king?

Yes, it is true that Grace and Diana were better known than you or I, but surely not better loved. For our Father loves us perfectly, each of His children, and that love is more precious than a scepter or a crown!

You are royalty, a princess, a child of the King if you trust the Lord with all your heart. If you have not taken this step or are unsure of your relationship to Him Who is your Father, please pray with me the words below.

PRAYER:

Lord God, King of Kings, I give myself to You, trusting You for all things, thanking You for washing away my sins with the blood of Your precious Son, Jesus. And now I marvel at the joy of being Your daughter—the daughter of the King! Amen.

20.

TODAY'S SCRIPTURE:
For God so loved the world, that he gave his only begotten Son, that whosoever believeth in him should not perish, but have everlasting life. (John 3:16, KJV)

Recently I heard a shocking statistic: Fifty-four percent of Americans not only cannot recite John 3:16, they are not the least bit familiar with it! Think of that.

"For God so loved the world . . ." For more than half of us in the United States, those words elicit only a shrug, an I-don't-have-a-clue look, a reaction of utter ignorance and indifference. So when someone holds up a sign at a sports event with the words "John 3:16" scrawled in letters big enough to read across the stadium, at least half the people cheering at the game don't automatically think, "Oh, yeah, that's the one that starts 'For God so loved the world.' "

"Fourscore and seven years ago . . ." (the Gettysburg Address, Abraham Lincoln).

"Now is the winter of our discontent . . ." (*Richard III*, Shakespeare).

"Listen, my children, and you shall hear . . ." ("Paul Revere's Ride," Henry Wadsworth Longfellow).

"When in the course of human events . . ." (The Declaration of Independence).

"I am the Lord thy God . . ." (The Ten Commandments).

The above are famous beginnings. When I hear them, my heart begins pumping with emotions: the thrill of a brief but magnificent speech; excitement as a curtain is raised; pleasure from familiarity with a favorite story set to verse; the weight of a heavy but courageous decision; awe.

Still, the one which energizes me to the core of my being, which makes me tingle with expectation for the words that follow is the beginning of John 3:16: "For God so loved the world . . ." I include it here in the King James Version as a reference, if it's the wonderfully familiar version you memorized as a child. And, if it is new to you, won't you hide it in your heart—today?

PRAYER:

Lord, thank You for so loving the world—and me—that You gave Your only Son, so that by believing in Him I will not perish, but will have everlasting life. Amen.

21.

TODAY'S SCRIPTURE:
Come to me, all you who are weary and burdened, and I will give you rest. (Matthew 11:28, NIV)

Some days I am weary. Bone weary. Emotionally weary. Creatively weary.

Even at my age—my twenties—I can tire out to a point where I tell a friend I need to escape from my household, my responsibilities, my life, because "they're killing me." It's an exaggeration, sure, but it conveys how I feel. Do you know what I mean?

On those days this simple verse from Matthew helps me. Reading it (or remembering it in my heart) is like heaving a great sigh. It's a hug. A gentle stroking through my hair with my head in my Father's lap.

The irony is that the verses which come next are challenging—they require a certain mental, emotional and spiritual agility to comprehend and respond to. But I'll get to those in the next meditation. For now let's just rest together.

PRAYER:
Father, hold me today as I come to You, weary and burdened by life's work and worry, and give me the rest You so generously promise. Amen.

22.

Come to me and I will give you rest—all of you who work so hard beneath a heavy yoke. Wear my yoke—for it fits perfectly—and let me teach you; for I am gentle and humble, and you shall find rest for your souls; for I give you only light burdens. (Matthew 11:28–30, The Living Bible)

For years as a high school and college student I had struggled with not only my deafness but other obstacles as well. I was very demanding of myself, thinking I had to overcome them on my own. I became disappointed—in myself, in others, in the world around me. I was carrying a heavy burden, or working beneath a heavy yoke, and I was also lonely at the same time. I was, frankly, very, very discouraged.

Then one day I saw a painting that gave me great comfort. It showed Jesus holding a young man in His arms. You may have seen this picture. The young man has a look of agony and disappointment on his face.

Well, when I saw that picture, I could relate to what the young man felt! His expression reflected what was in my heart, the sense of hopelessness I felt. On the bottom of the picture was the Bible verse I quoted above.

So the entire work of art consisted of these elements: a compassionate and strong-looking Jesus tenderly holding in His arms a young man who could be going through the same pain I experienced, plus a Scripture that invites us to give our troubles to Him. And instantly I understood: No one on this earth can overcome the obstacles he or she faces without the help of Jesus. No wonder we become so tired and discouraged; we try to do it on our own when He is offering us a better way, His way. What touched my heart so deeply on the day I saw this picture was the realization that His unconditional love holds me completely safe and secure.

I chose the Scripture from The Living Bible for today's meditation. If you are a careful reader, you will notice that I included the verse from yesterday but added the next two verses. I love how The Living Bible explains His yoke— "for it fits perfectly." Just the fact that it is called a "yoke" makes it sound heavy, like an instrument of great burden. But immediately He assures us that the perfect fit will make it easier, a joy to wear—and to learn from ("and let me teach you"—He is so gentle and humble that He teaches us only if we *let* Him!).

Yes, a rest for my soul! Yesterday I wrote of being bone

weary, emotionally and creatively so tired that I needed to escape. Today I take comfort in His promise not only to give me rest but to provide a yoke which fits so perfectly that it is a light burden. Our yokes—yours and mine—are perfect fits, because they were made especially for you and me!

This gives me energy. It makes me ready to tackle my day.

PRAYER:
Lord, I accept Your yoke with its perfect fit designed just for me—my body, my temperament, my skills, my desires, my needs. Thank You for providing me with rest and challenging me on! Amen.

23.

TODAY'S SCRIPTURE:

Do not say, "I'll pay you back for this wrong!" Wait for the Lord and he will deliver you. (Proverbs 20:22, NIV)

The first Christmas after John and I were married, a very dear friend of mine gave me a letter tucked inside a Christmas package. For reasons I still don't understand, she filled this letter with hurtful words about how my marriage wouldn't last. (How many things look good on the outside but turn out to be bad on the inside? Unfortunately, the same can be said for a few people.)

Before this painful experience, I had trusted her. I needed a woman mentor—what young bride doesn't?—and I shared with her some of the inevitable pain and confusion I felt as a young bride. Now she was predicting that my marriage would end.

Eventually, I turned to godly women for their gentle help, built on God's Word as revealed in the Scripture and in their hearts, which were attuned to Him through a life-time of seeking Him daily.

I didn't cut this woman completely out of my life. That would have been a form of retaliation, I feel. However, I did not trust her and never called on her again for advice and support.

This proverb is about forgiveness as well as waiting on the Lord to deliver us from people who harm us. Think of the people who have hurt you. If you have tried to "pay them back," has it truly added any satisfaction to your life? I doubt it. I hope and pray you will leave justice to the Lord. As mentioned elsewhere in the Bible (see Deuteronomy 32:35 and Psalm 94:1), vengeance is God's prerogative, not ours.

PRAYER:
You, Lord, are the only One Who can mete out justice. Save me from the temptation to do this job of Yours. Help me to forgive, rather than to repay. Amen.

24.

Make no friendship with an angry man; and with a furious man thou shalt not go. (Proverbs 22:24, KJV)

Did you know that fishermen don't put tops on crab baskets? That's because crabs are a self-regulating population: If one captured crab starts to climb up the side of the basket, the other crabs will reach up and pull it back down.

Some days during my reign as Miss America, I felt like one of those trapped crabs. People would hold me back, or—worse—pull me down.

As I began to adjust to the reality of being the first Miss America with a disability, I realized that my dream had changed. Now that I possessed the crown and title I had sought, I had a new goal. Like one of my heroines, Helen Keller, who used her powerful influence to bring hope and light to the world, I thought perhaps the way to achieve my goals of helping deaf people might be through legislation. But it didn't take me long to lose patience with the political system of Washington. Sure, some wonderful people are involved with government, but politics seemed to be more a system of trading favors than the serious business of improving people's lives. Everywhere I turned, eager to shine my light, I was met with controversy and criticism.

Why are some people so quick to dwell on the negative? Though I am as human as anyone else, I don't want to dwell on life's miseries. I want to seek out the bright, the right and the positive things.

But as I traveled and spent more time with people who had negative attitudes, I was distracted from looking for the positive, and my dream slowly shriveled and died. I had great ambitions, but I learned that even Miss America can't change people's hearts unless they are willing to be changed.

Oh, it certainly wasn't all bad. I received letters from mothers whose deaf children were encouraged and empowered by my success, but their hearts were young and optimistic. Those who were world-weary looked at my twenty-one-year-old face under the crown and pronounced me young and idealistic.

But the Lord was always in control, even when things looked bleak to me. He brought me two friends who helped me accomplish my goal. They both had positive perspectives. We launched a huge campaign about the early detection of hearing loss, and we worked with the Alexander

Graham Bell Association in providing $77,000 in scholarships to bright deaf students.

PRAYER:
Today, Lord, please direct my path away from angry, negative people and lead me to people who can help me realize my dreams, which are dedicated to You. Amen.

25.

If you are pleased with me, teach me your ways so I may know you and continue to find favor with you . . . (Exodus 33:13, NIV)

Although these are the words of Moses, I can relate to them.

Moses wanted literally to *see* God. How often I have felt that desire! Like Moses, who had experienced a "taste" of God, the more I get the more I want.

Like a good parent, God gave Moses detailed instructions for chiseling out the two stone tablets which were to replace the ones that Moses had broken in a fit of righteous anger. God then told Moses to go to the top of Mount Sinai and present himself there alone.

Moses followed the instructions of his Heavenly Father to a *t*. He chiseled the tablet, awoke early and climbed the mountain. And there God rewarded him with his heart's desire. According to Exodus 34:6–8, God passed in front of Moses, proclaiming, "The Lord, the Lord, the compassionate and gracious God, slow to anger, abounding in love and faithfulness, maintaining love to thousands, and forgiving wickedness, rebellion and sin. Yet he does not leave the guilty unpunished; he punishes the children and their children for the sin of the fathers to the third and fourth generation." Moses bowed to the ground at once and worshiped.

I believe God can be seen only as He chooses to reveal Himself. Will you watch for Him today?

PRAYER:
Today I pray as Moses did, Lord, that, if You are pleased with me, You will teach me Your ways so that I may know You and continue to find favor with You. Thank You for revealing this truth and Yourself to me today. Amen.

26.

TODAY'S SCRIPTURE:

But to keep me from being puffed up with pride because of the wonderful things I saw, I was given a painful physical ailment, which acts as the Devil's messenger to beat me and keep me from being proud. Three times I prayed to the Lord about this, and asked him to take it away. His answer was, "My grace is all you need; for my power is strongest when you are weak." I am most happy, then, to be proud of any weaknesses, in order to feel the protection of Christ's power over me. I am content with weaknesses, insults, hardships, persecutions, and difficulties for Christ's sake. For when I am weak, then I am strong. (2 Corinthians 12:7–10, Good News for Modern Man)

Do you believe God causes your physical ailments?

I don't have a definitive answer for this question (which people love to argue about, by the way!). But I can tell you with certainty that I sense that God *allowed* my deafness.

He permitted this to be a part of my life, and I understand why.

If I were not deaf, I might be proud. And, if I were proud, I might be separated from God. And, if I were separated from God, I might not experience the protection of Christ's power over me.

So I am convinced that being deaf is my lot in life, that it is part of God's plan for me, and I am content with it.

What infirmities do you suffer? Could God have permitted you to have them? If so, why?

PRAYER:
Thank You, God, for my infirmities and ailments, both now and in the future, and for Your grace, which is sufficient, in fact abundant. Amen.

27.

TODAY'S SCRIPTURE:
For he himself is our peace, who has made the two one and has destroyed the barrier, the dividing wall of hostility, by abolishing in his flesh the law with its commandments and regulations . . .
(Ephesians 2:14–15, NIV)

Minorities or people who are oppressed or people who are different and misunderstood by others—often they are divided among themselves on how to live in the world around them, with the very people from whom they feel cut off. Maybe they disagree on how militant to be. Some members of their group want peaceful civil disobedience to effect change; others want violence. Perhaps they disagree on how to get laws passed—with threats or with the proverbial carrot on a stick. Often they simply disagree on perception—how they want to be viewed by the rest of society, which sees them as different.

Such is the case in the deaf community. There is disagreement over using sign language, which is understood only by those hearing people who have consciously chosen to learn it, or using speech. I choose the latter. I can read lips and usually tell what people are saying. Then I answer in my voice rather than using my hands to sign.

A hearing person may think this is a no-brainer. But actually it takes quite a risk to speak when you wonder if your voice is going to come out squeaky (and you can't hear it, so you don't know!). The fear of sounding foolish is a strong motivator (think how many people are afraid to sing!). That's why many deaf people choose to communicate by sign language.

Of course, no one's way is the *only* right way. Both ways are right. It's a legitimate choice.

This verse reminds me that, no matter what our differences, we are bound together by the Lord's peace.

When I was much younger, I struggled with this issue of how to communicate. In fact, I still struggle with fitting into the worlds I straddle—the deaf community and the hearing community, the lip-reading community and the signing community. But I've learned that struggle is okay. And reading this verse helps to put into perspective that we are all one family, no matter how we "hear" or speak. It helps me to love others, even those with whom I disagree.

PRAYER:

Father, thank You for giving us our differences, for making us unique human beings within one family, Your precious family. Help me to focus today on the qualities we share as Your children. Amen.

28.

The Lord is my shepherd; I shall not want. He maketh me to lie down in green pastures: he leadeth me beside the still waters. He restoreth my soul: he leadeth me in the paths of righteousness for his name's sake. Yea, though I walk through the valley of the shadow of death, I will fear no evil: for thou art with me; thy rod and thy staff they comfort me. Thou preparest a table before me in the presence of mine enemies: thou anointest my head with oil; my cup runneth over. Surely goodness and mercy shall follow me all the days of my life: and I will dwell in the house of the Lord for ever. (Psalm 23, KJV)

Who can improve on this beautiful expression of God's care and comfort and provision?

I looked this up in several versions and finally chose the old standby, which many of us probably memorized in childhood.

It always gave me joy to recite it then, and it still gives me joy today. Like many things in life that seem commonplace, we sometimes overlook it for trendier sayings and verses and thoughts. But this one is so complete that I offer it to you along with plenty of silence in which to ponder its beauty and magnificence.

PRAYER:

Jesus, my Shepherd, I am Your lamb. I follow You everywhere with trust and contentment. Thank You for leading me beside still waters, for leading me to places of comfort and safety. Thank You for restoring my soul, for renewing my spirit. Thank You for leading me in the paths of righteousness for Your name's sake, for pointing me down the straight and narrow path You have chosen for me. I know that I often walk through the valley of the shadow of death, and truly I fear no evil, because of Your holy presence. Thank You for preparing a table before me, even where my enemies can see. And thank You for anointing my head with oil. You are so giving and so generous that my cup runs over. I am certain that goodness and mercy will be mine forever. And I pray to dwell with You in Your house through eternity. Amen.

29.

TODAY'S SCRIPTURE:
And on the seventh day God finished his work which he had done,
and he rested on the seventh day from all the work which he had
done. (Genesis 2:2, RSV)

Our Heavenly Father celebrated by resting when He finished His work.

I look back over my own life and wonder if I do this
too.

The truth is, I don't do a good enough job of resting—
rejuvenating my energies, surveying what I have accomplished and getting ready for the next task.

When I was in high school and college, I would take
time to read my Bible when I finished my homework. It was
a reward to me. God refreshed my heart by sharing His
words of encouragement. And, afterward, when I would lay
down to sleep, I could see the stars dancing with their lights
through my window. That sight reminded me that I was

finished for the day, that seeing those lights was my reward from Him for doing what He asked me to do.

To be honest, I don't take the time to rest and celebrate the end of an accomplishment now that I'm older. I'm a busy wife, I have demands on me as a public speaker, I'm the mother of two dogs (don't laugh).

God is waiting for me at home, just as He did when I was a child, but too rarely do I take the time to rest with Him. And I pay for it by lying down at night and feeling that something is missing.

This verse is a good reminder that we must model our behavior after God's perfect example. We must rest as He did.

PRAYER:
Forgive me, Father, for not disciplining myself to take time to rest with You. I understand that You created me for Your glory. You have dreams for me. I must be ready. And proper rest is a part of Your perfect plan. Amen.

30.

TODAY'S SCRIPTURE:
For I know the plans I have for you, declares the Lord, plans to prosper you and not to harm you, plans to give you hope and a future. (Jeremiah 29:11, NIV)

I'm constantly amazed at the realization that God *really* has a plan for me (and for you!).

For example, I know that God placed in my heart the desire to dance. In addition, He placed in my body the ability. Not only the desire and ability to move my feet and my body, but to do it in a way that brings honor and glory to Him.

He placed me in front of a television audience of forty million people to dance to the Christian song, "Via Dolorosa." I'm referring, of course, to the talent competition in the Miss America pageant.

Many people may think of a "beauty" (I call it "scholarship") pageant to be a silly thing. I don't. And the reason is not only my belief in the principles of the pageant, but what I learned about God and His power from that experience.

I believe He paved the way for me to do that dance. He wanted others to experience the message of that music. He wanted me to dance for His glory. I'm absolutely convinced He used the entertainment vehicle we take for granted—television—to convey His message of love and grace. His *plan* was for me to be on that stage. I could feel it as I danced. And I sense that plan to this day.

Of course, He wants me to *enjoy* the art of dancing, too. Like a wise parent (the wisest), God knows I would not be too motivated unless what He planted in my heart to accomplish was enjoyable.

As a woman in my twenties, I'm too young to know what else He has planned for me. But I consider it my responsibility to watch, to wait and to find out. I think it would be selfish and self-centered for me to ever think that, after all He has given me and done for me, I should strike out on my own, as if I have the ability to cut a path for myself as wonderful as the path He has planned.

But, unfortunately, that's the message in our culture—*you* can do it! For years, men got that message from society; now women get it too. Not that men and women aren't capable. Of course we are. And people who don't know the Lord are often very accomplished human beings. But for those of us who know to Whom we belong, we have a special responsibility to acknowledge His role in our life—planning it, shaping it, directing it. If we will let Him.

PRAYER:

Lord, forgive me when I am too selfish to realize that Your dreams for me are better than any I could have for myself. Help me to see Your plan for my life and to fit into it willingly. Guide me and direct me throughout the day. Amen.

31.

Before I formed you in the womb I knew you, before you were born I set you apart; I appointed you as a prophet to the nations. (Jeremiah 1:5, NIV)

I'm proud to be known as a patriotic American. It's what drew John and me together in the first place. He was working in Newt Gingrich's office. I was traveling around the country as Miss America, speaking out on values such as chastity, which resonated among politicians at the local level and members of Congress who were trying to return this nation to its moral roots.

Among the most interesting people I met during that year, 1995 to 1996, was Elizabeth Dole. What a gracious lady! To me she possessed the traits of an American woman of *any* century. Are you surprised I would say that? Don't be. Think about it. In her you have a true southern belle, yet a Harvard graduate. You have a woman so accomplished she has served in cabinets of U.S. presidents, yet she's not known for her great skills in the kitchen. Her beauty and grace and charm are part of an already impressive résumé. When she is on a stage, she commands attention because of her intellect, her style, her wit and her courage—characteristics we saw in other great women throughout history, like Dolley Madison, Harriet Tubman and Eleanor Roosevelt.

This is not meant to be an unabashed tribute to Mrs. Dole. All people have faults. She is a human being, so no doubt she has them too.

My point is simply this: When people such as Mrs. Dole rise to the surface, we should look to this verse from Jeremiah. For the Lord God is bringing leaders into our midst. Will they be successful? Only the polls can tell us that, because people—the voters—are fickle. But some of them—and I'm certainly not in a position to say specifically whom these people might be—are God's emissaries, His ambassadors. It is our job as people seeking God's will to be on the lookout for such people.

For, as it says in Jeremiah, people are set apart. We see this in our culture. People are targeted for specific jobs; sometimes they are even targeted for ridicule. But in God's perfect world, there are people He has chosen to serve on His behalf, to work for Him in our society.

Will one of these people be you? Perhaps as a volunteer? Perhaps as someone who speaks out on an issue that God places on your heart? Maybe as someone who speaks up in front of people as you feel God is leading you?

This is a completely nonpartisan commentary, because I believe God is not confined to a party label or to any other box. However, I'm convinced that He searches for people to serve Him in the public arena, the public square. And, because He formed us in our mothers' wombs, because He knew us before we were born, He has selected each of us for *something.* But for what?

I urge you to search your heart to see if God is leading you to speak out as a citizen, to participate in the process of democracy, to stand up for character, to vote your conscience, to serve Him with your loyalty—to the nation in which He formed you in your mother's womb and delivered you for service.

PRAYER:

Lord God, today I come to You with a heavy heart on a tough subject. Many people are pulling at me from different directions. I know You called me to be a citizen, but does that mean I must be an activist within a party? I feel You want me to be an activist for the Truth, Your Truth. Please help me to discern what that Truth is and how it applies to the society in which You have deliberately placed me. Amen.

32.

TODAY'S SCRIPTURE:
*Gray hair is a crown of splendor; it is attained by a righteous life.
(Proverbs 16:31, NIV)*

Confession time.

I promised early in this book to be real and honest with you, my reader. And today's Scripture gives me the opportunity—in spades!

It's not easy for a former Miss America to admit that, as I grow older, I must work harder to keep myself in good shape and still look beautiful.

As I read this verse, I'm reminded that physical beauty is skin deep but that real beauty comes from within. It comes from knowing, trusting and serving the Lord.

It draws lasting praise, the only applause that's really worth seeking.

As I read this verse, I think of Barbara Bush, a woman not known for great physical beauty yet greatly loved by people for her inner strength, a form of beauty far greater than slim hips or a smooth complexion.

I have been privileged to meet many famous women, some of them in political circles. And, when I do, I take notice of how they handle themselves. I will pass along to you that the ones who have qualities that are lasting are the ones whose qualities begin far beneath their skin—that begin in their hearts.

As I come to the second half of my twenties, this is the type of beauty I now seek. The one that Proverbs refers to, the one that God reveres. For He is the only audience that really matters!

PRAYER:
Dear Lord, reset my priorities if they need adjusting, so that I understand what is worthy in Your eyes, You Who created real and lasting beauty. Help me to seek that beauty, which springs from my heart, which is placed there by You. Amen.

33.

TODAY'S SCRIPTURE:

Then I turned my thoughts to consider wisdom, and also madness and folly. What more can the king's successor do than what has already been done? I saw that wisdom is better than folly, just as light is better than darkness. (Ecclesiastes 2:12–13, NIV)

It was my second date with John. How well I remember this important milestone!

We were in Washington, D.C., where he worked on Capitol Hill. He took me to one of the most sentimental locations in the nation's capital, the Lincoln Memorial.

This is the large, rectangular structure on the District of Columbia side of the Memorial Bridge, spanning the Potomac River. The building connects the North and the South, Virginia and the capital city of our country. It's a grand site, not to be confused with other locations: The Jefferson Memorial is round, and the Washington Monument is a tall obelisk in the center of the Mall, which stretches between the domed Capitol building and the pillared memorial dedicated to Abraham Lincoln.

Personally, I cannot think of a more godly president than Lincoln. So, naturally, I was impressed by John's patriotism, his loyalty not only to America but to God. I was thrilled that we were visiting this site together, standing (literally!) at the feet of Lincoln.

And so as we stood inside the memorial, gazing up at the statue of the president sitting in an enormous chair, John read to me the words of the Gettysburg Address. I looked at John, having no idea this man was my future husband, and I saw tears in his eyes.

He said to me, "You see, Abraham Lincoln said that our nation was born and then it seemed to be dying during the Civil War. But the nation was born again."

I was surprised by this. I asked what he meant.

And John, a student of history, explained: "When I studied this speech, I learned that Lincoln was reading his Bible on the train as he rode to the Gettysburg battlefield to deliver his hastily written speech. He recognized the analogy between Jesus and our nation. Jesus died. And then He was born again. And that was to be our nation's future."

PRAYER:
Lord, thank You for resurrecting not only Your Son but our nation from a horrible time of trouble. You must care about

94

us a great deal to grant us such grace. And, likewise, You must love me a great deal to place me as a citizen in such a nation. I pray that I will live up to this awesome responsibility. Please lead me to people of greatness. Open my eyes to their wisdom. Amen.

34.

Two are better than one, because they have a good return for their work . . . (Ecclesiastes 4:9, NIV)

One of the most difficult decisions of my life was the timing of my marriage to John.

I felt called to marry him because I loved him and because I was sure that, as a couple, we could serve God more fully than as two single people. There are times when one plus one adds up to more than two. This seemed to be one of those times.

But society says I should have waited until I finished college. This was a tough call!

I cannot give anyone advice about when to marry the man of her dreams, the person she feels God has made for her.

But I can say this with full authority: God will be with

you as you make this important decision. That is, if you ask Him.

I will not claim that He writes in the sky the answer to this dilemma. That did not happen for me. But He will bless your decision as you seek His will. He communicates in a subtle, almost indiscernible way. And yet it is the perfect way!

It can be frustrating at times, especially for a decision as important as this. Our hearts are full and our bodies are aching for our loved one. We are human, exactly as God made us to be. And, no, the answers generally don't seem to be crystal clear.

But I can assure you that He honors our attempt to seek Him in this decision. He will demonstrate His appreciation and His approval of your trust and faith. And you will be glad you sought him. For His guidance is sovereign, even if it does not match with what your aunt says, or your teacher or your best friend. Seek it for this most important of all decisions, second only to your choice to follow Jesus as Lord and Saviour.

PRAYER:

My Lord, when my time comes to make this all-important decision, please be there with me to discern who You have in mind for me and to determine Your will about the best time to marry the person You have formed for me. Thank

You for Your faithfulness in this important matter. It means so much to me. And I promise to follow Your wishes in this matter even if it means timing I feel is wrong. I trust You and want to live the life You have planned for me. Amen.

35.

So give your servant a discerning heart to govern your people and to distinguish between right and wrong. For who is able to govern this great people of yours? (I Kings 3:9, NIV)

Who better to honor with a verse from I Kings than Dr. Martin Luther King Jr.? In my opinion, he is one of the greatest Americans who ever lived. I look to his words for wisdom and for strength and for dignity. I know many people who honor Dr. King with framed photographs of him on their wall. Many schoolchildren have memorized his famous "I Have a Dream" speech.

I am white. However, the things that Dr. King stood for and spoke for transcend race. He used God's love to influence humanity, to touch the hearts of Americans and to foretell a better society that could be enjoyed not only by black Americans but by Americans of every other color along the spectrum.

What made Dr. King such a great hero to people of all

races, I believe, was his ability to see that God's love over-flows—it seeks nothing in return but loyalty. It seeks nothing but speaking out, standing up, being counted for what is right.

He spoke of a society that does not glorify one race while suppressing another (which has been the case in our country, I'm sad to say). He knew that all men are endowed by their Creator with certain rights.

And the greatness of Dr. King was that he personally knew the Creator. He was not just an orator; he was a believer. His Father is my Father. And, for that reason alone, he is my brother, no matter the color of his skin.

PRAYER:
Heavenly Father, thank You for creating us with differences You planned and You blessed. Help me to see the world as You want me to see it, celebrating the differences You created. I want to do my part to heal the problems between the races, and I look to You for my help. Show me an opportunity to be of service to You in this way. Amen.

36.

TODAY'S SCRIPTURE:
Do not curse the deaf or put a stumbling block in front of the blind, but fear your God. I am the Lord. (Leviticus 19:14, NIV)

I don't intend to lay a guilt trip on people who have misunderstood a deaf person—either because our speech pattern sounded a little strange to your hearing ears or because you looked upon us as different and therefore not worth knowing. However, I think there's a reason the Lord puts such a strongly worded admonition in the Bible.

My theory is that it's because we deaf people have been made by Him. And, assuming you as a reader are part of the hearing world, so have you!

In other words, I think God wants us to realize that He is the Creator and that we have no right to mistreat or abuse *any* part of His Creation.

And so this is all I will say on this subject. However, speaking for many deaf people I know, I consider this verse worth meditating on today.

PRAYER:

God, You are so holy and good. We cannot understand how You have created us, only that You did it with love and for our best interests. Forgive the scandalous behavior with which we sometimes treat Your Creation, and show us how to love one another. Amen.

37.

TODAY'S SCRIPTURE:

The law of the Lord is perfect, reviving the soul. The statutes of the Lord are trustworthy, making wise the simple. (Psalm 19:7, NIV)

I have found in my life that a transformed life is not a matter of scholarship, but of discipline.

This simple yet profound verse tells us that the Scriptures contain all we need to know to revive our souls, our families and our societies.

When we are troubled as people or as a nation, we should turn to the Scriptures, which, when held up as a standard, never fail. What I find fascinating, as a layperson who seeks to understand the Word of God, is that, with Scripture, the deeper you dig, the deeper the meaning. While many other works of literature—great books, speeches, poems—often appear profound, perhaps even the result of sound thinking on the surface, when you dig deeper, so many times you find they are shallow.

Not so with the Word of God. Never so with the

Scriptures. For His law is perfect, and His statutes are trustworthy.

PRAYER:
Thank You, my Lord, for providing me with a sound doctrine based on both logic and grace. I know I can depend on it, and I love You for inspiring it. Amen.

38.

TODAY'S SCRIPTURE:
And as for you, brothers, never tire of doing what is right.
(2 Thessalonians 3:13, NIV)

A role model for today's woman, no matter what her age, is Ruth Graham.

Any biography of the wife of Billy Graham will show you insight into her godly life. Yet it has not been all roses!

Her famous evangelist husband is a world traveler. He is personally known by heads of state, by many of the most powerful people in the world. Relationships like that take time to build and establish. And his crusades themselves are time-consuming. They require enormous work and effort. And, although Billy Graham has a large and capable staff, I know that he personally has devoted a great deal of his own time to their preparation.

So, of course, much of his life has been spent far away from home, away from Ruth. She has accompanied him on occasion but, more often than not, she stayed home and raised their five children.

This means she had to make decisions. When a daughter needed a curfew, Ruth set it. When a son needed guidance about attending a college, Ruth provided it. When a daughter looked for help in selecting a career, there was Ruth, dishing it out. When a child needed academic encouragement, Ruth was the one to take care of the need.

But she is quick to say that her guidance was always inspired by the Lord, by her daily walk with Him in the mountains of North Carolina, where she and Billy raised a family and directed a worldwide ministry.

Her life may seem easy, but it has been tiring, she writes and is quoted as saying. Yet she never literally tires of it. Oh, to be honest, I'm certain she's gone to bed with a backache, has quit washing dishes because her feet hurt, has stopped talking in social situations because her voice has just plain given out.

But she has never been weary in a permanent sense, only temporarily. For Ruth Graham has always been convinced that the work that she and her husband do as a committed team is well worth the energy and the attention and the incredible time she contributes. This is because she knows it is "right." She knows it is work assigned to them by the Lord. And she knows that she and Billy were chosen to do the job.

So it is with all of us who walk in His path. Our work

may not be known around the world, but it is known by the One Who cares.

PRAYER:

Father, thank You for giving me a worthwhile task to occupy my time and attention. If it is not clear to me, clarify it. If my will is not strong enough to accomplish it, strengthen my will. Today, I pledge myself fully to Your work, because it is "right." Amen.

39.

For there is not a thing that God cannot do. (Luke 1:37, Good News for Modern Man)

Mary, the mother of Jesus, was a young, inexperienced country girl and yet she became God's obedient servant by believing that, with Him, nothing is impossible.

What simple—yet profound—faith!

I think of how today's woman so often intellectualizes all that she knows, transforming the easy to know into the difficult to understand by trying to appear smart when wisdom would suit her so much better.

When I consider Mary, I have to come to grips with the choice that God made then—and apparently makes now. He searched the whole world for a young woman to bear His Son.

Who is He searching the whole world for today?

He, of course, really did not need Mary, or any other woman, for that matter, to accomplish His goal. However,

He had said in earlier Scripture that His Son, the Messiah, would be born of a woman, and, true to His Word, Jesus was. But God certainly could have accomplished His purpose in Jesus without Mary.

Instead, he chose to use her womb to carry His precious Son. Think of it! What an honor for Mary. And yet what a confusing time for such a young, naive girl.

I am touched whenever I think how much faith she must have had to realize that the baby she was carrying was truly from the Lord. For in those days she surely would not have had the education our students get today, and so perhaps a condition such as pregnancy was terrifying to Mary.

How gracious is the Lord to let us in on the secrets of His world! To utilize us to fulfill His purposes! To choose us to carry out His plans!

PRAYER:

Gracious Lord, thank You for providing a Saviour and for honoring all of womankind by delivering Him to the world through the body of a gentle, young woman whose life we can emulate with the guidance of Your Scripture. Amen.

40.

TODAY'S SCRIPTURE:
Whether you turn to the right or to the left, your ears will hear a voice behind you saying, "This is the way; walk in it." (Isaiah 30:21, NIV)

When I first got involved in the deaf world right after I graduated from high school, I was thrilled. Unfortunately, I felt like I met the wrong group of deaf people. They told me I was not a part of their community, because I used my voice to communicate with the hearing world.

I grew up a lot because of that experience. Here I was wanting so much to be a part of something! I was looking for people like myself, people who could understand me, my opportunities and limitations as a deaf person. So I became discouraged, because I felt left out so often in the hearing world and now I was being told I was not part of the deaf world either.

Of course, as I matured I recognized that their attitude was a form of "political correctness," doing something in a prescribed way to please a certain group. It was a lot like being snubbed by the crowd you want to belong to. It hurt me a lot, but it also had a positive impact: It drove me into the arms of our Heavenly Father.

He comforted me when I read the Bible. I read the story about Thomas, the disciple we often call Doubting Thomas, because he had to see Jesus' wounds as proof that He had come back to life after being buried in the tomb.

Jesus said, "Blessed are those who have not seen and yet have believed" (John 20:29). I realized that the same could be said of those who have not heard Him—literally heard. I felt this revelation was God's way of saying to my heart, "You, Heather, are My child. Nobody can hear or see Jesus, so they all have a handicap, not just you. My children only become a part of my family when they choose to believe My Son."

We can hear our Father in heaven with our hearts. God never fails to communicate with us, but we often fail to communicate with Him. Sometimes we make decisions without listening to God for His advice. He knows the way to make our life successful, and yet we too frequently ignore Him. I hate to say it, but it's true. It's as though we are deaf in our hearts. And that's impossible, because He communicates with us in our hearts if we let Him. We may be deaf or hard of hearing in our ears, but we choose to be deaf in our hearts. And it's a shame, because He wants to speak to us, to guide us, to lead us.

Some people use the word "dumb" to describe deaf people. It's a misuse of the word "mute," which means nonspeaking. But I say we *are* dumb if we try to accomplish our dreams without God's help! It's so foolish and unnecessary.

Ask yourself whether you are trying to hear God's voice with your ears or your heart. It's a question you must answer some time in your life, and I hope you will do it today.

PRAYER:

Father, sometimes I don't make wise decisions, and I know that You have been disappointed in me. I fail to include You and that is the reason I pay the price of failure. Sometimes I try to use the wrong part of me to hear You. Yet I know I have the ability to hear from the heart You have given me. Please speak to me through my heart and allow me another chance to hear Your precious direction for my life and to experience Your perfect love for me. I want to hear You with my heart from now on. Amen.

41.

Everyone who competes in the games goes into strict training. They do it to get a crown that will not last; but we do it to get a crown that will last forever. (I Corinthians 9:25, NIV)

I love using the Bible-study book called *Thru the Bible* by J. Vernon McGee (Thomas Nelson, 1983). McGee explains that "in an athletic event, only one can come first. But in the spiritual race all of us can win the prize if we are getting out the Word of God. The awards that God gives won't swell your bank account down here and remain here when you leave; they will be for your eternal enrichment" (page 43).

I'll never forget my feeling when I turned around at the end of the runway during my Miss America crowning moments. For a few seconds, I could see the contestants' faces. They were really excited for me, and I was thankful for their kindness. But later that night, and even now as I write this meditation, my heart ached for them. They had worked hard to get there. They, too, dreamed of walking down the runway holding the Waterford scepter and wearing the Miss America crown. I felt like I had robbed them of their dreams, because only one of us could be crowned.

This Bible verse comforts my heart, and it means a lot more to me as I think back on those moments right after the crown was placed on my head. I still have it and travel with it in a special wooden box. I visited Spain in 1998 for the Starkey Hearing Aid Company. While I was there, I showed the crown to deaf children I visited. (Because Spain has a queen, the Spanish children called me a ballerina, rather than a queen. That distinction made me laugh!) I would invite the children to gather around, and then I would open the wooden box and gently lift out the crown. Their eyes got big, and they all wanted to touch it. Even the boys wanted to place the glittery crown on their heads. The looks on their faces said "awe." The crown inspired them to dream of big pursuits.

After I finished performing my ballet, I shared the Good News with them. I explained to them that Jesus is the key to my success. And, more important, with Jesus as our Saviour, we are part of God's family. We are no different from other people without disabilities in God's eyes.

I believe this gave them hope. In Spain, deaf people are isolated. They are told that they can't accomplish as much as hearing people. For example, as children they are taught that they can't aspire to be doctors or politicians or hold other occupations of influence. I really believe that perspective will change one day because of improved technologies, which give deaf people more opportunities to be part of the hearing world. But the important thing is, with God's help, anything is possible. I challenged them to look up to God for His support and guidance.

My crown has helped me to bring encouragement to others who have struggled with their obstacles. The sparkling crown reminds all of us that we will receive a crown of joyful life in God's kingdom forever. This is the *real* crown we are all "in the running" for.

PRAYER:
Father, I was given a crown of sparkling stones, but I can't imagine receiving a crown of thorns as Jesus did. He accepted it with no complaints and died on my behalf. My sins were the cause of Jesus dying on the cross. Because You and Your Son Jesus are one, then I caused Your death as well. Forgive me for crowning You with thorns. Your mercy and grace are so hard for me to understand. You could have ended my life and destroyed me in a second, but You didn't. Instead, You crowned me with life. Your love is amazing. Thank You for giving us the precious gift of our lives. Amen.

42.

And the Lord God said, "It is not good that the man should be alone; I will make a help meet for him." (Genesis 2:18, KJV)

I have been married to John for two years. Becoming a married woman was a huge change in lifestyle for me. I no longer go out and spend money on my own, even if the item I want is on sale. I include John in the decision. In this way, my marriage trains me for a relationship with God. I am God's helper and must consult Him about my decisions, just as John and I consult each other. We are accountable to each other as we are accountable to God.

As a wife, I feel God calls me to be John's helper. During his campaign for secretary of state of Georgia, we traveled tens of thousands of miles, zigzagging across the state, shaking people's hands, hearing their concerns, talking about solutions.

The campaign was a mixed experience. Sometimes I had to endure hearing opponents lie to the crowd about themselves and about my husband. We had to work hard to get messages out to the Christian people we met along the way. It was important for them to know that one who shared their values wanted to work for them. Several times I volunteered to give testimonies at the churches we visited, because I felt God called me to help His plan for John.

At one point during the months of campaigning, I just collapsed. I even began to hate and resent the campaign. I had lost all sense of privacy in my home. Campaign workers were everywhere. I couldn't use the telephone whenever I wanted to talk to someone. I could no longer use the downstairs office because it had been taken over by campaign workers. So I bought a notebook computer and converted an upstairs bedroom into an office for myself, a place where I could be alone to think of what lessons to share with readers of this book.

I retreated into my office. I even began missing some of the political events, because when the campaign workers were gone I could find some peace and quiet at home.

But then I felt the Lord nudge me into being John's helper. He needed me to be out there on the campaign trail as my husband's companion. One confirmation of this came when John mentioned to me that the last time he gave a certain speech, it was terrible. Yet when I was by his side, he had felt good about giving his speech. I think my being there helped to lift his spirit.

It's not easy to be a helper in the political world, because it isn't very beautiful in spirit. It's a lot like the "real world" in that way—also ugly at times. But John feels strongly that God calls him to be a part of it. And I am told by the Bible that God made me to be my husband's helper. My place is by his side.

Has God called you to be anyone's helper? If not yet, maybe He will later in your life. You must ask God to prepare you for this special role. He promises to walk with you and, based on my experience, I can say He lives up to this promise completely!

PRAYER:

Sometimes I miss my old world, Father, but I know You made me for a purpose. Help me to find that purpose and to fit into it with graciousness and a heart of thanksgiving. Being single has its rewards, but so does marriage. I trust You to be with me as I fit into whatever role You have in mind for my life. Amen.

43.

TODAY'S SCRIPTURE:
For the Lord God is a sun and shield; he bestows favor and honor. No good thing does the Lord withhold from those who walk uprightly. (Psalm 84:11, NRSV)

No marriage is perfect, and no husband and wife have the ideal relationship at all times.

In yesterday's meditation I wrote how exasperated I could become during my husband John's campaign for secretary of state of Georgia. When I met him John worked in the political world, in the office of Newt Gingrich, Speaker of the U.S. House of Representatives. At that time John was on staff, not an elected official. Now John feels God calling him to a life of public service in the political realm. And this means getting elected, subjecting ourselves to the scrutiny of the press and the voters. Because I love our country and its democratic system, I know it's worth the trouble.

But for the first-time campaigner—namely, me—it can

be exhausting, intimidating and disruptive to a life of service to God, which requires a certain amount of calm and peace (two rare commodities in my life as I write this book but which I hope you can enjoy while you use it to meditate upon the Lord!).

I have found perfect strangers in my home at all hours. They are wonderful, dedicated people, and I've grown to know many of them well. But they are "here," and there's no denying that their presence in my living room, my kitchen, my dining room—namely, everywhere!—is incredibly invasive.

Yet I read in God's Word how He wants me to live. And I see that He wants me to help my husband in his life's work. And, because I believe God's promises, I know that no good thing does He withhold from those whose walk is blameless.

It's one thing to read such comforting words. But I can say without hesitation that there is truth behind them. God blesses me and bestows grace on me to endure things I never thought I would be capable of doing.

I often miss the peace and quiet of our life before politics. It was a time when John and I had so much freedom and privacy in our house. But I also know that this is a sacrifice which God helps me to endure. And, in fact, His blessings far outweigh any discomfort.

Are you sacrificing freedom and privacy for your family? Do you understand that this is part of God's plan for couples and families? Do you realize that God blesses you for your endurance and walks with you as You follow His perfect plan for your life?

PRAYER:

Dear Father in heaven, I give You my burdens. Take away my selfishness and self-centeredness and replace them with a desire to serve You by being a good spouse. Thank You for Your promise to help me with this almost overwhelming task. Amen.

44.

This is how the birth of Jesus Christ came about: His mother Mary was pledged to be married to Joseph, but before they came together, she was found to be with child through the Holy Spirit. Because Joseph her husband was a righteous man and did not want to expose her to public disgrace, he had in mind to divorce her quietly. But after he had considered this, an angel of the Lord appeared to him in a dream and said, "Joseph son of David, do not be afraid to take Mary home as your wife, because what is conceived in her is from the Holy Spirit. She will give birth to a son, and you are to give him the name Jesus, because he will save his people from their sins." All this took place to fulfill what the Lord had said through the prophet: "The virgin will be with child and will give birth to a son, and they will call him Immanuel"—which means, "God with us." When Joseph woke up, he did what the angel of the Lord had commanded him and took Mary home as his wife. But he had no union with her until she gave birth to a son. And he gave him the name Jesus. (Matthew 1:18–25, NIV)

Yesterday I wrote about a kind of unsung hero in the political world—the spouse who campaigns publicly but, in private, may be stressed almost beyond description. It's a lifestyle many people have, whether they are in the public eye or not. You may be one of them.

Today I'm focusing on one of the Bible's most extraordinary unsung heroes, Joseph, the earthly father of Jesus. Very little is known about this humble and trusting man, and yet I have always been impressed by his quiet heart.

Based on this Scripture, we can be certain Joseph knew he had a huge responsibility. Yet we have no record of his taking any credit for what must have been an almost overwhelming behind-the-scenes duty—preparing Jesus for manhood. I doubt that he asked for anything other than this "supporting role" in the world's most magnificent drama. He seemed willing to follow the Lord's directions completely, including sacrificing his own needs for marital intimacy in order to fulfill the prophecy about the Messiah.

How can we be sure that Joseph knew God personally? The answer to that lies in Joseph's reaction to the dream. When one of God's angels appeared to him while he was sleeping, Joseph recognized Whose instructions the angel was giving, and obeyed to the letter.

Who has the Lord placed in your life in a supporting role? Perhaps there's a neighbor or an aunt or a grandparent or a teacher. Is there an unsung hero who gets little credit for influencing you but who deserves your thanks?

Heavenly Father, thank You for the people You place here on earth to parent us, either formally or informally, with their wisdom and guidance. Make me aware of those people around me, and nudge me today to thank them for their support. Amen.

45.

A wife of noble character who can find? She is worth far more than rubies. Her husband has full confidence in her and lacks nothing of value. She brings him good, not harm, all the days of her life. She selects wool and flax and works with eager hands. She is like the merchant ships, bringing her food from afar. She gets up while it is still dark; she provides food for her family and portions for her servant girls. She considers a field and buys it; out of her earnings she plants a vineyard. She sets about her work vigorously; her arms are strong for her tasks. She sees that her trading is profitable, and her lamp does not go out at night. (Proverbs 31:10–18, NIV)

Do you know the wonderful thirty-first chapter of Proverbs, which describes the traits of a wife of noble character? If not, I hope you will acquaint yourself with it. I consider it to be the blueprint for how to live as a married woman. I cannot claim that I live up to it, but I certainly try. Today I have quoted approximately half of it. Tomorrow I will quote the rest.

One godly woman whose name and face come to mind is Maria, the former nun who becomes a wife and mother in the musical *The Sound of Music.* Although many talented actresses have played the part on stage, I remember Julie Andrews best, who played the role in the movie.

The story is based on the Von Trapp family, who escaped the Nazis during World War II by "climbing every mountain" and following their dream of freedom. Eventually, they wound up in Vermont, where they established a ski resort, probably reminiscent of their former life in Austria. I think they were greatly inspired in their successful escape by Maria, who was high-spirited and full of fun and adventure. It takes not only a very focused person like her but one who is willing to trust God and take some risks in life to pull off the kind of maneuver they did to outwit the Nazis. Maria probably made a good nun, but—assuming the movie is a fairly accurate portrayal—she made a wonderful wife and mother. She inspired her family to try new things, not to let anything stop them, to walk away from a bad situation and to trust that God would deliver them to a better place.

The Proverbs 31 woman is strong and hearty. She is a hard worker, rising early and staying up late. As such, she is a role model for her children, both the boys and the girls. She is certainly no shrinking violet or wimp. She doesn't whine about having a lot of responsibility. In fact, she welcomes it. She makes business decisions with confidence.

Her husband can rely on her good judgment. She apparently is successful, because she manages enterprises such as a vineyard. And she oversees people, such as servants (to whom she is generous by providing them with portions of food). It amuses me that radical feminists so often misunderstand the Bible. They think the women described in it are not strong—either physically, emotionally or spiritually. How wrong they are! I can think of so many women described in the Bible whose practical strength and wisdom are admirable no matter which millennium we live in. Consider these (and, if you're not familiar with them and their stories, I would encourage you to look them up in the Bible): Esther, Ruth, Naomi, Solomon's bride, Elizabeth, Abigail.

Tomorrow we will look at the rest of Proverbs 31 and talk about one of the strongest women I know, although she cannot lift a finger nor walk even one step.

PRAYER:

Dear God, I am so grateful for women (and men) who serve as role models and who inspire me to a life of strength and boldness and service. Forgive me if I ever contribute to the world's mistaken view that a person of either gender can accomplish much of anything through idleness or the weakness of spirit the nonbelieving world often admires. Help me find the strength to be a person of noble character like the wife described in Proverbs 31. Amen.

46.

In her hand she holds the distaff and grasps the spindle with her fingers. She opens her arms to the poor and extends her hands to the needy. When it snows, she has no fear for her household; for all of them are clothed in scarlet. She makes coverings for her bed; she is clothed in fine linen and purple. Her husband is respected at the city gate, where he takes his seat among the elders of the land. She makes linen garments and sells them, and supplies the merchants with sashes. She is clothed with strength and dignity; she can laugh at the days to come. She speaks with wisdom and faithful instruction is on her tongue. She watches over the affairs of her household and does not eat the bread of idleness. Her children arise and call her blessed; her husband also, and he praises her: "Many women do noble things, but you surpass them all." Charm is deceptive, and beauty is fleeting; but a woman who fears the Lord is to be praised. Give her the reward she has earned, and let her works bring her praise at the city gate. (Proverbs 31:19–31, NIV)

This passage is the continuation of the Bible's view of the wife of noble character, as described in the thirty-first chapter of Proverbs.

As with yesterday's passage, it describes a woman of true strength and beauty. She has confidence ("she can laugh at the days to come"). Her husband is well respected (and "he praises her"). In fact, her husband thinks she's the greatest! (When he praises her, he says, "Many women do noble things, but you surpass them all.") Her children are proud of her and say so (they "arise and call her blessed"). She is a wise and loving counselor ("faithful instruction is on her tongue").

So why should this woman be given the reward she has earned and be praised publicly ("at the city gate")? According to verse 30, she is a woman "who fears the Lord."

Fearing the Lord is her wise and understanding response to the awesomeness of God.

I can think of no better example of this kind of wise— and, yes, *strong*—woman than Joni Eareckson Tada. In case you haven't been exposed to this incredible woman, she's a quadriplegic who lost the use of most of her body in a tragic diving accident as a teenager. And, although she's confined to a wheelchair, she is (in my estimation) the very model of strength.

Joni's strength comes not from her muscles but from her heart. She "fears the Lord." That is, she knows the Lord personally, respects His awesome power, has experienced His healing love and understands that her correct response to His call to her is to be obedient.

Now, this does not mean Joni is always serious. In fact, if you've never heard her on the radio or seen her appear in person, then you don't know she's one of the most jovial commentators speaking out today. Sometimes her humor makes me laugh out loud! She is full of fun.

Joni is also not afraid to share the fact that, because of her disability, she sometimes gets down and depressed. I respect her for being honest about that. If she denied it, I don't think I could trust what she says about the Lord.

By the way, Joni is married. She did not let her handicapped status stand in the way of a loving and committed relationship to a man who adores her in return.

I encourage you to study the biblical traits of a wife of noble character. If you are female, ask yourself if you should aspire to be like her. If you are male, find out how closely she fits your impression of the ideal wife.

PRAYER:
Lord God, You are so awesome, and I too rarely acknowledge Your power. Please hear my prayer today as I humble myself before You—a way of "fearing" You. Thank You for tucking into Your Word this inspiring passage describing the wife of noble character. It teaches me that "charm is deceptive, and beauty is fleeting; but a woman who fears the Lord is to be praised." Amen.

47.

Then Queen Esther answered, "If I have found favor with you, O king, and if it pleases your majesty, grant me my life—this is my petition. And spare my people—this is my request. For I and my people have been sold for destruction and slaughter and annihilation. If we had merely been sold as male and female slaves, I would have kept quiet, because no such distress would justify disturbing the king." (Esther 7:3–4, NIV)

Esther is one of my favorite heroines in the Bible. She had the courage and conviction to do the right thing for her people, the Jews. I see many applications for what she did in today's world.

In a nutshell, what happened is that she allowed herself to be mentored by an uncle to become queen. Her Jewish ancestry was kept hidden from the king; one of her husband's royal officials was plotting to destroy the Jews.

Esther put herself into a position of influence and power. Eventually, the king offered to grant her a wish, even to divide his kingdom in half and give it to her. But Esther thought instead of her people, whose annihilation was imminent. She asked her husband to spare them. As it turned out, the king didn't even know about the plot. He was enraged and had the guilty man executed. But the role played by Esther was key, because she risked her own life. She could have infuriated her husband by exposing the vicious plot of one of his trusted aides. But she was prepared to pay the price—perhaps even her own life—for speaking out for justice.

There are women today who take personal risks to speak out for what is just and fair. I think of Shirley Dobson, for example, who chairs the National Day of Prayer, which occurs the first Thursday of every May. Calling for prayer for our nation may sound fairly innocuous to you. However, she goes a step farther. She asks people to pray that our nation's leaders' hearts will change. She wants people to see that abortion, the killing of babies, is an annihilation just as surely as the one Queen Esther was speaking of, which would have wiped out her race of people, the Jews.

Are you taking risks and making your voice heard on issues that are meaningful to you? Should you?

PRAYER:
Father, grant me the wisdom to know where my voice could be effective and the courage to speak up and be counted. Amen.

48.

The girl at the gate said to Peter, "Aren't you also one of the disciples of that man?" "No, I am not," answered Peter. (John 18:17, The Good News Bible)

Peter is so easy for me to relate to because he's human and vulnerable to the kinds of weaknesses we all suffer from.

For example, in this passage he is hovering outside the high priest's courtyard, where Jesus is being questioned on the night of his several (and unfair) "trials." The next day Jesus will be crucified on the cross. Yet on this momentous occasion Peter's awful words are being recorded for all eternity.

Like us, when we do the same thing, Peter has an excuse. He knows his life is at stake. He might be found guilty by association. So when the girl asks his identity, he denies being one of Jesus' disciples. Peter goes on to make two more such denials. And, if you recall the story, a rooster crows right after the third time he denies his relationship to Jesus—a sign Jesus himself predicted to Peter, who made a promise of loyalty that Jesus knew he would not be able to keep.

It's shocking that Peter would do this, even outrageous. We all like to think that if Jesus were among us today in the flesh, we would be proud of our relationship to Him and outspoken in our loyalty.

Yet, He's with us in spirit, and we don't honor that as consistently as we should. We are rarely fearful for our lives, but we are fearful we will lose something we hold up to be almost as precious as our lives: our reputations. We think if we say we are one of Jesus' "disciples" people will laugh at us or write us off as irrelevant or even ignore us. They won't consider us to be cool. We won't be popular. We won't have their respect. We won't have their "love," which is based on senseless things if it's not based on Jesus.

Still, I have to admire and respect Peter. He's a true hero to me. Does this surprise you? It's because he did not let his mistake stop him from preaching the Gospel. Only a couple of months after this horrible night, during which he denied Jesus three times before the rooster crowed (in other words, before morning), Peter began preaching the good news that Jesus died for our sins.

It's hard to recover from such a mistake. Many times we beat up on ourselves so much that we never get around to doing the right thing. We just keep going on and on about what a jerk we've been. I love Peter because he didn't stay down on himself. Instead, he pulled himself up after making a terrible mistake, which is what we all should do.

PRAYER:

Jesus, forgive me when I deny my relationship to You. I do it more often than I like to admit by the way I behave, the way I talk, the way I treat others. I don't always act like someone who carries You in my heart, and for that I am ashamed. Please help me to pull myself up from such a mistake and carry on like Your servant Peter did. Amen.

49.

Now the earth was corrupt in God's sight and was full of violence. God saw how corrupt the earth had become, for all the people on earth had corrupted their ways. So God said to Noah, "I am going to put an end to all people, for the earth is filled with violence because of them. I am surely going to destroy both them and the earth. So make yourself an ark of cypress wood; make rooms in it and coat it with pitch inside and out . . ." (Genesis 6:11–14, NIV)

Talk about a man who subjected himself to ridicule!

You may have seen Bill Cosby's bit about Noah. It's hilarious, not only because Cosby rolls his eyes around in such a comic way as he imitates Noah in his routine, but because, when you think about it, the idea of getting such instructions from God is really pretty wild!

Cosby's monologue about Noah makes people laugh. But I imagine people in Noah's day really *did* laugh at him. They probably thought he was a first-class fool.

First, they didn't believe that what they were doing was evil. Second, they didn't take time from their wicked behavior to get to know God personally, so they didn't know He disapproved. And, third, they had no idea that God was powerful enough to cause a flood which would destroy them.

If they thought of God at all, they probably put Him in a "box" like so many people do today.

In fact, we do it ourselves when we don't stop to think what God *can* do if we provoke His anger. We often dwell so much on the loving aspects of God that we ignore evidence that He may be disappointed in us.

I would like to think that, if I heard the voice of God telling me to build an ark with very exact dimensions and then to gather a male and female of every creature on earth, I would do it. But I know I would be laughed at—and not because I'm a comedian. I would look foolish to the unbelieving world.

And yet when we take precautions and make choices as God instructs us, we are doing just that. If we are careful not to participate in what the crowd wants to do, if we turn down opportunities to do something we know will displease God, no matter how much it tempts us, if we walk away from a situation that "everybody's doing"—then we are hearing God's voice, following His instructions and subjecting ourselves to ridicule.

I believe He honors our efforts to follow Him, and He gives us the strength and courage to do the right thing even in the face of laughter.

PRAYER:

Holy Father, thank You for guiding me. I know people will make fun of me today for following You, but I pray that You will give me the strength and courage to do it anyway. I am not afraid of their laughter. But I am afraid of Your wrath. Please put Your loving arms around me as I do my best to please You and return Your generous love. Amen.

50.

TODAY'S SCRIPTURE:
Fear none of those things which thou shalt suffer . . . be thou faithful unto death, and I will give thee a crown of life. (Revelation 2:10, KJV)

I have mentioned the crown for my head that I was given as Miss America. It's quite elegant and glittery. Did you know that I also have a crown brooch, which I wear on my lapel?

I read recently that a town in Missouri was being sued by the Americans for Civil Liberties Union (ACLU) for having the Christian fish symbol as part of their town seal. This story really saddens me. I think it's wonderful for people to be able to symbolically tell others that they are believers in Christ.

We do this all the time by what we wear. Our clothing is a personal message to the world of who we are, our attitudes, our beliefs.

I proudly wear the Miss America crown on my lapel just as I'm sure many of you wear a cross around your neck or a fish symbol on an article of clothing, such as a T-shirt (I wear those too!). But, when we wear such symbols, we are sending more than a signal to the world about our beliefs. We are giving people a reason to expect certain behavior from us.

Haven't you seen someone who's drunk wearing a cross and then felt terribly embarrassed? When they got dressed, they made a decision that was about far more than accessorizing an outfit—they made a statement saying they love the Lord.

If we are wearing a cross or a fish and we are doing something that doesn't honor the Lord, then we have reduced a sacred symbol to nothing more than a piece of jewelry.

PRAYER:

Jesus, I know that You died on the cross for my sins. And the cross which is in my jewelry box is a symbol of that sacrifice and not just a piece of jewelry. Please forgive me if I ever forget this important distinction. Amen.

51.

TODAY'S SCRIPTURE:
Let your gentleness be evident to all. The Lord is near. (Philippians 4:5, NIV)

It was Kathie Lee Gifford who challenged me to be a Christian in the spotlight.

Although I appeared on *Live with Regis and Kathie Lee* only a few days after being crowned Miss America, she saved this precious piece of advice for another occasion. We both were making appearances at the Super Bowl. She was there to sing "The Star-Spangled Banner."

Kathie Lee, herself a devout Christian, knew I carried Christ in my heart, and she also knew I was drawing public attention because I was Miss America. She realized the novelty of my being deaf added another dimension. As we waited backstage, she quoted a Bible verse to me about praising the Lord, and I realized I could be more open about my faith in Jesus while I traveled around the country meeting people as Miss America.

But the Scripture above speaks of "gentleness," not necessarily a trait we exude when we are in high-profile or powerful places.

For example, I remember meeting the president and first lady. Mrs. Clinton encouraged me to be true to myself and to stand up for my beliefs. After our ten-minute meeting, she led me into the Oval Office, where President Clinton showed me his desk. It had belonged to John F. Kennedy. I said something about my dad and grandparents owning an Ethan Allen furniture store, and then the president and I shared a laugh. Suddenly, the press entered the Oval Office to take pictures. I realized that I was standing next to the most powerful man in the world.

I definitely felt unworthy, but I don't know if I felt gentle.

The times when I believe I exuded the most gentleness were when I met with schoolchildren and told them my story. One of the best moments during my reign as Miss America was when I met a boy who was both deaf and blind, and I helped him to caress the crown. I think that was a moment when I connected, not by being famous but by being gentle.

Lord, place in me the desire to be gentle, to demonstrate the gentleness You have placed in me as one of Your fruits of the Holy Spirit, and to always be a gentle reminder of Your saving love for Your people. Amen.

52.

TODAY'S SCRIPTURE:

Stop your anger! Turn off your wrath. Don't fret and worry—it only leads to harm. (Psalm 37:8, The Living Bible)

Another true confession from one who hates to admit this particular truth: I fret a lot, and it definitely causes harm. In fact, it's my greatest handicap. So this is the verse I always go back to when I catch myself fretting and becoming angry. It challenges me to discipline myself.

Can you be honest with yourself and think of your greatest handicap? I'm not asking you to admit it out loud to anyone, just to yourself and, of course, to God.

It's hard to admit these things (especially to readers of a book!), but I think that when we identify our greatest weakness, we are halfway home to licking the problem.

Rather than write a lengthy meditation today, I am going to challenge you to spend a few minutes thinking of what might be your greatest handicap and then asking the Lord to help you overcome it.

PRAYER:

Dear Heavenly Father, You made me the person who I am. You created me with certain weaknesses, and yet You challenge me to overcome them. I believe You gave me these weaknesses to draw me closer to You. And so that's what I'm doing now. I'm asking You to help me with the weakness I have admitted to You. I pray that You will make clear to me exactly what it is, why I do it and how I can overcome it. If You have a Scripture which I can hide in my heart to help me with this weakness, please reveal it to me someday, so that I may dwell on it when I am tempted. Thank You for Your faithfulness in giving me the strength that I request. Amen.

53.

TODAY'S SCRIPTURE:

Wives, submit to your husbands, as is fitting in the Lord. Husbands, love your wives and do not be harsh with them. Children, obey your parents in everything, for this pleases the Lord. Father, do not embitter your children, or they will become discouraged. Slaves, obey your earthly masters in everything; and do it, not only when their eye is on you and to win their favor, but with sincerity of heart and reverence for the Lord. Whatever you do, work at it with all your heart, as working for the Lord, not for men, since you know that you will receive an inheritance from the Lord as a reward. It is the Lord Christ you are serving. Anyone who does wrong will be repaid for his wrong, and there is no favoritism. Masters, provide your slaves with what is right and fair, because you know that you also have a Master in heaven. (Colossians 3:18–25 and 4:1, NIV)

These verses apply to the Christian home—to family members, to employees, to employers.

They tell us some instructions that are hard to carry out. Our sinful nature makes us want to flee from such truths and realities. Yet the Lord knew we needed to hear these things, so He made sure they got written down in this precise manner for us.

I believe the instructions address those things we as fallible human beings have the most trouble doing, and so the Lord provided us these reminders and analogies. For example, I think many women—myself included—have to work hard to be submissive. And I think many men have to work hard at being loving. Children have to work hard at being obedient. Employees have to treat their earthly employers as if they were serving Christ. And employers must model the Heavenly Master in their treatment of their employees.

These are difficult to do but necessary if we are to work effectively together as a family and in employment situations.

Psychologists speak of functional and dysfunctional families. It's obvious by their labels which is the desirable type. If we followed to the letter the admonishments in this passage, we could achieve the kind of functional relationships that many people spend money trying to achieve through therapy and other self-help activities.

I think the underlying message in these verses is to set straight our priorities. If we accept that *all* of our relationships should reflect the Lord by modeling how we are intended to relate to Him and He to us, then this passage is easier to understand and live by.

Father, help me to understand and—more importantly—to live by this difficult passage. My sinful nature makes me want to turn my back on Scriptures like this and deny them. But I know You gave them to us for our own good, to help us to get along better and to be more effective as family and employment units. And so You ask us to model our relationships with others after our relationship with You. Thank You for this explicit instruction. Amen.

54.

TODAY'S SCRIPTURE:

For all of us make many mistakes. Anyone who makes no mistakes in speaking is perfect, able to keep the whole body in check with a bridle. (James 3:2, NRSV)

All my life I have been taught that Jesus is the only perfect man and that no one can ever live up to Him. And then I come across a Scripture like this one.

Either this verse is meant as sarcasm or it is meant to give us hope that we too can achieve the perfection which Jesus attained by being God in the flesh.

This is daunting, isn't it? Yet I believe that there is a reason why so many verses are devoted to telling us to depend on God for our strength. He promises to be there with us as we reach for the ultimate goal: perfection.

Whether we ever achieve it seems to be addressed in the sentence that reads: "We all stumble in many ways." In other words, not only do *all* of us stumble, we do it in *many* ways.

It is so comforting to me personally, as a sinner, to realize that not only does God promise to walk with me as I strive for perfection, He also tells me that it is nearly impossible to achieve. That is the kind of straightforward information from God which makes Him trustworthy and completely believable.

PRAYER:

Heavenly Father, I will try hard to be perfect, but I know I am likely to fall short. Thank You for encouraging me to try, but thank You also for warning me that in all likelihood I will stumble in many ways. It is easier to trust You and to lean on You, because You are realistic and honest with me about my journey. Amen.

55.

The king said to me, "What is it you want?" Then I prayed to the God of heaven, and I answered the king, "If it pleases the king and if your servant has found favor in his sight, let him send me to the city in Judah where my fathers are buried so that I can rebuild it." (Nehemiah 2:4–5, NIV)

If you are an architect or an engineer or anyone who likes to create things, especially with your hands, then the Old Testament Book of Nehemiah is for you. It's chockfull of wisdom about so many aspects of life, in addition to the art and science of building.

First, some background. Nehemiah was the cupbearer to the king. This was a trusted and highly responsible position, because enemies were always trying to kill the king and take away his kingdom. So the cupbearer's job was to select and taste the king's wine. (If the cupbearer dropped dead after such a tasting, it meant the wine had been poisoned. How about that for a high-risk job?)

Nehemiah, a Hebrew living in a foreign land, knew that his "hometown" of Jerusalem was defenseless because the wall around the city had been damaged so heavily. He requested a leave of absence from his job with the king to return to Jerusalem and oversee the rebuilding of the wall.

Reading the story, we see many examples of Nehemiah using good judgment in managing both a building project and managing people. For example, he kept confidential his plans until he knew whom he could trust. He delegated responsibility, which not only was a more productive way of rebuilding the wall, it encouraged a spirit of teamwork. He asked for the help of professionals to consult him as he made his plans and carried them out. He expected setbacks; he was realistic enough to know that he would encounter opposition, and he built this into his time schedule. He set boundaries, not allowing the priorities of others to steer him off course or divert his attention. He took time to celebrate small accomplishments along the way with his many helpers, giving credit where credit was due.

In short, Nehemiah established and followed sound principles for project management.

But the real hero of the book is God Himself.

The story teaches that God never calls us to do something unless He enables and empowers us to do it. So when God has a task for us, He walks along beside us and helps us to accomplish it. Like Nehemiah, God wants us to finish our work—not just "somehow"—but triumphantly!

Do you have a big task ahead of you? Is it work? Is it school? Is it a personal task you need to get done? Let's say you have been meaning to write a certain report, or apply for a job, or move to a new location.

Have you questioned whether the task is what God is calling you to do? It may be something that your teacher or employer wants you to do, but you don't see the need for it. Ask yourself if, out of obedience to God, you should do it out of obedience to your employer. And, if you are sure the task is what God wants you to do, have you asked for His generous help and support?

PRAYER:

Heavenly Father, I want to be more like Nehemiah. People could depend on him to do the right thing, and I want people to feel the same way about me. I want to be productive. But I need Your help and guidance. I need You to show me the direction I should go, and I need for You to show me the individual steps to get there. Please break down my task for me into bite-size pieces, which are not so overwhelming, and lead me in carrying out each one. And, if the task I want to tackle is not what You want me to do, please steer me clear of it entirely. Amen.

56.

TODAY'S SCRIPTURE:

It will be as though a man fled from a lion only to meet a bear, as though he entered his house and rested his hand on the wall only to have a snake bite him. (Amos 5:19, NIV)

Talk about having a bad day! Reread today's Scripture passage, and go ahead and laugh out loud.

But the truth is that the lesson of Amos is very serious.

Amos was a prophet sent by God to His people to warn them of the kind of trouble they were getting into. The people had become prosperous and decadent. They were doing wicked things. They had become selfish, even destructive.

For example, rich people were taking advantage of the poor. They were self-indulgent, lounging around on their couches instead of working. They acted religious, but they were only faking it—it was all an act!

Amos, speaking for God in his role as a prophet, tells the people they must seek God, establish a personal relationship with Him and live within the boundaries of that new life. In other words, they must behave themselves!

Amos warns them that, if they don't repent and find God, all manner of horrible things will happen to them. He gives examples such as drought and famine, plagues and earthquakes. They will not be able to avoid the terrible fate that will fall on them. But it will be their own doing, because they've become so wicked.

Does any of this sound familiar?

Are we sitting around wasting time on foolish things such as too much television, instead of making good use of our time? Are we claiming to love the Lord and yet not living up to our promises to Him? Are we doing things we know displease the Lord?

One of the main messages of Amos is that we are accountable for our actions and our attitudes. I must examine mine every day, and I encourage you to do the same, starting now.

PRAYER:

Lord, I come to You with a heavy heart, because I know that, although I may not be as wicked as these people mentioned in the Bible, I do things which displease You. I want to take seriously my relationship with You. This means I must be accountable for my behavior and my thoughts. I give these to You now, this very minute, and ask You to purify them, so I may live for You and better serve You. Amen.

57.

TODAY'S SCRIPTURE:
Both hands are skilled in doing evil; the ruler demands gifts, the judge accepts bribes, the powerful dictate what they desire—they all conspire together. (Micah 7:3, NIV)

It is a mixed blessing to see the government of the United States up close.

I am so proud to be an American, of this nation founded upon principles of religious liberty. People came here from all over the world to be free to worship as they please, to earn a living in the way that best suits them, to enjoy a system of justice and freedom for all.

I am one of those people who chokes up when the band strikes up *"The Star-Spangled Banner"* or I see the flag going up a flagpole. I have shared earlier in this book that one of my most memorable dates with John was the time he took me to the Lincoln Memorial in Washington, D.C., and read to me some of the inscriptions engraved on the wall. I want to be active in the process of protecting our freedoms, including from the tyranny of people who are not godly.

Most of the people in our government are fine, hard-working citizens, I am sure, but I also think there are a few corrupt people, like the ones mentioned in today's Scripture passage. People who are in positions of leadership should expect to be held up to public scrutiny, because they have so much influence. For example, if a teenager shoplifts, he may get a light sentence to teach him a lesson. But if a judge shoplifts, he should lose his position on the bench, probably even his license to practice law.

I am appalled at the number of people who don't think our political leaders should be moral leaders, and yet moral leadership is a biblical principle. It dates back to the Old Testament, as shown in verses such as this one from Micah.

People look at our leaders and they think: I can aspire to greatness like him or her. They also think the opposite: If he or she can do it and get away with it, why can't I?

The irony is that people in positions of leadership can ask God's forgiveness and receive it, no more and no less than those of us who are followers or who are relatively unknown. They have the same opportunity to be forgiven by God as we do. And do you know what? God not only forgives, He completely *forgets*. Our transgressions are completely washed away by the blood of Christ.

Study these words in Micah 7:9: "Because I have sinned

against him, I will bear the Lord's wrath, until he pleads my case and establishes my right."

PRAYER:

Righteous and Holy Father, whether I am a powerful person or a humble person just trying to get by in life, I know I am accountable to You for everything I do. I ask forgiveness for my many sins, and I trust that You will forgive them as I trust in Jesus as my Lord and Saviour. I understand it is You and not myself Who can change my life. Amen.

58.

TODAY'S SCRIPTURE:

And there were in the same country shepherds abiding in the field, keeping watch over their flock by night. And, lo, the angel of the Lord came upon them, and the glory of the Lord shone round about them; and they were sore afraid. And the angel said unto them, Fear not: for, behold, I bring you good tidings of great joy, which shall be to all people. For unto you is born this day in the city of David a Saviour, which is Christ the Lord. And this shall be a sign unto you; Ye shall find the babe wrapped in swaddling clothes, lying in a manger. And suddenly there was with the angel a multitude of the heavenly host praising God, and saying, Glory to God in the highest, and on earth peace, good will toward men. (Luke 2:8–14, KJV)

One of my favorite songs is the wonderful Christmas hymn "O Holy Night." It depicts the night when Christ was born. The glory and grandeur of that special night are captured in the lyrics, like in the Scripture above.

I was only fourteen when my parents got a divorce. I needed a peaceful feeling in my heart at that tender age and stage in my life, as do many young people during the breakup of their homes and family unity. I've talked to children about the divorce and shared how much this event affected me. I know what they are going through. It hurt me like it hurts them.

Since that event, "O Holy Night" has always given me a peaceful feeling deep inside.

When I first understood its meaning, I was at a candle-light service with my church family. All the lights had been cut off, and we had switched to candles. I love a Christmas candlelight service. It's so natural, so moving. After all, on the holy night of Jesus' birth, the only lights were candles and the glow from heavenly bodies such as the moon and the stars.

On this particular night at my church, I saw the candles flickering and the quiet, peaceful expressions on everyone's faces. They also glowed, not only from the candlelight but from the joy of full hearts.

And, suddenly, my own heart was overflowing with love for Jesus. It felt like the ocean's rough waves suddenly becoming calm amid silence, with the stars above sprinkling God's love down on me.

I decided that the song was a gift to me. Just as the Christ child is a gift to all of us from our Heavenly Father.

This was a time when my earthly parents were creating turmoil. But my Heavenly Father was filling my heart with peace and love.

And it was a time when the baby Jesus was real to me. He was only a baby but still a child like I was then, a child who would go through joys and heartaches, growing pains and triumphs.

I felt secure, a feeling that still comes over me when I know "O Holy Night" is playing.

PRAYER:

Thank You, Heavenly Father, for the holy night when Christ was born. Thank You for the moment when I felt my heart overflow with Your Son's love. Thank You for loving me just as much as You love Him. Amen.

59.

O God, my heart is ready to praise you! I will sing and rejoice before you. Wake up, O harp and lyre! We will meet the dawn with song. I will praise you everywhere around the world, in every nation. For your lovingkindness is great beyond measure, high as the heavens. Your faithfulness reaches the skies. His glory is far more vast than the heavens. It towers above the earth. Hear the cry of your beloved child—come with mighty power and rescue me. (Psalm 108:1–6, The Living Bible)

I was aboard an airplane making one of the most important flights of my life when I read the book *Jonathan Livingston Seagull,* written by Richard Bach.

I was headed for Atlantic City, New Jersey, and the Miss America pageant. I was representing my home state as Miss Alabama. It was definitely a soaring experience! Here I was flying thirty thousand feet above the ground on my way to an event that I felt I had prepared for all my life. I could relate to the seagull not only because I was flying like he was but because the seagull could see the sand below him on the beach.

That bird's-eye view brought me to my childhood memories of carefree days near the Gulf of Mexico when I was a little girl. My family vacationed there nearly every weekend at the beach. I spent hot summer days building sand castles and playing in the waves. I loved to watch the water recede and leave a lacy foam on the sand.

I could see the warm, sparkly sand from my height as a little girl. But now—as I soared high above the earth on my way (I hoped and prayed!) to capture the Miss America crown—I could imagine the view from the perspective of the seagull. He seemed so regal and brave. He gave me a hopeful spirit.

As the plane landed I felt inspired to try my best to become Miss America. Whenever I see a copy of the book or think of *Jonathan Livingston Seagull,* I remember that flight.

PRAYER:
Lord, You populate our earth with special people, even birds who inspire us to soar to new heights! Thank You for Your Holy Book, the Bible, but also for the secular literature we find that sometimes provides us with experiences which live on forever in our hearts and memories. Amen.

60.

When Jesus was twelve years old he accompanied his parents to Jerusalem for the annual Passover Festival, which they attended each year. After the celebration was over they started home to Nazareth, but Jesus stayed behind in Jerusalem. His parents didn't miss him the first day, for they assumed he was with friends among the other travelers. But when he didn't show up that evening, they started to look for him among their relatives and friends; and when they couldn't find him, they went back to Jerusalem to search for him there. Three days later they finally discovered him. He was in the Temple, sitting among the teachers of Law, discussing deep questions with them and amazing everyone with his understanding and answers. His parents didn't know what to think. "Son!" his mother said to him. "Why have you done this to us? Your father and I have been frantic, searching for you everywhere." "But why did you need to search?" he asked. "Didn't you realize that I would be here at the Temple, in my Father's House?" (Luke 2:41–49, The Living Bible)

165

Sometimes I think young people don't get enough credit.

It's true that there have been some tragedies lately—like the increase in teenage criminals, especially the hard-core ones who murder their teachers and classmates. But, for the most part, teenagers in America are still good kids.

Today's youth have a lot of extra pressures. Many of these are self-inflicted, of course. For example, if some teens weren't so violent, schools would be safer. I know of kids who are actually afraid to go to school.

But other pressures are inflicted by society, by a nation that values materialism too much and therefore pushes kids too hard to succeed. Parents sometimes draw the conclusion that money equals success. Their kids pick up on this notion and feel pressured in school, not so much from the love of learning but for the love of what material success will do for them. They want faster cars or bigger computers or more CDs. These are enjoyable, sure. But they don't have true, lasting value, the satisfaction that comes from a relationship with Jesus Christ. Wherever I speak, I emphasize that wrong values are dangerous. They seem to multiply with each generation.

However, let's focus on the many good parents out there and the good kids they are raising! There are plenty of functional families who don't make the news. I'll give you three examples. In each case, the ideas and the implementation come from the kids.

I know a family in Maryland who includes homeless

people in their Thanksgiving dinner. They don't worry about how well (or poorly) these people are dressed as they share this holiday meal around their dining room table. The important thing is that they are giving of themselves, providing hospitality.

A family in Texas wraps presents for mentally disabled people and delivers them on Christmas Eve at the local school. They do this in lieu of a self-indulgent evening. This activity involves finding the gifts and wrapping them, organizing the event every year with the school personnel and then having the discipline to do it when so many other families are having fancy parties.

There's a family in Illinois who sponsors a nondrinking New Year's Eve party. They play games, wear party hats and watch the Times Square ball drop at midnight, but with no alcohol and no rowdiness.

Like Jesus at twelve years old (see today's Scripture), the youth who put together these activities are "where they should be." They are beginning to take their place as leaders. They have a vision for how to live. And, like Jesus in the temple talking to the elders, they are forming lifelong habits that will translate into a lifestyle of right attitudes, healthy activities and service-oriented obedience to God.

PRAYER:

Jesus, I want to be like You in all that I do. Even as a youth, I want Your heart for God. As a grown person, I want Your wisdom, Your knowledge, Your love. And, someday when I'm preparing to die, I want Your courage. Please help me to find my way in this world no matter what age and stage of life I'm in. Help me to start that journey today. Amen.

61.

As is written in the book of the words of Isaiah the prophet: "A voice of one calling in the desert, 'Prepare the way for the Lord, make straight paths for him. Every valley shall be filled in, every mountain and hill made low. The crooked roads shall become straight, the rough ways smooth. And all mankind will see God's salvation.'" (Luke 2:4–6, NIV)

Yesterday's meditation was on how young people are often misunderstood and lumped together because of those who do harmful things that reflect on all youth, in many people's eyes. I listed examples of some encouraging things I've learned about the youth of America, ideas they have for giving to others—sharing, serving and leading.

Today I will focus on how youth can be evangelists. Yes, that's true!

People sometimes think of evangelists as Billy Graham or Luis Palau or other well-known ministers who stand in front of huge crowds and ask people to come forward and dedicate their hearts to Christ. That's certainly one form of evangelism but not the only kind.

People—including teenagers—can share their faith with others for the purpose of drawing others into a personal relationship with Jesus. In fact, they not only can, they *should.* Studies show that ministers simply cannot handle alone the workload of preparing sermons, administering all the work of a congregation, such as visiting people and managing a budget, and also bringing unsaved people to Christ. The job of minister has increased over the years. So laypeople, the folks who sit out there in the pews, have to lend their assistance to this vital work. And, guess what? According to the Bible, we're *supposed* to do it. We're all expected to be like John the Baptist ("the voice" mentioned in today's Scripture), who prepared the way for the Lord.

We can do this with one-on-one relationships. We can establish a close friendship with someone who is not saved, which means he or she doesn't have a personal relationship with the Lord—has not asked God for forgiveness for sins, does not understand or accept the great sacrifice made by Jesus on his or her behalf, does not worship and participate in the fellowship of believers.

Many people in the Christian "community" hang around only with other Christians. But there's a growing movement to encourage people—especially youth—to establish relationships with unsaved people that will develop into opportunities to share the Gospel. There's even a phrase for this: friendship evangelism.

This is such a serious part of your journey with Christ that I'm going to dwell on it for longer than usual today. (Remember how I promised early in this book that some meditations would be shorter and some would be longer? Well, this one will be longer, because the subject matter is so vital. "Growing" the Christian community with new believers is a big part of what we are all called to do. I hope you will devote the additional time today to meditating on this important responsibility.)

The point of friendship evangelism goes beyond just demonstrating how you live. Sure, if you're a Christian student (or adult), you show new friends that you watch the language you use, that you behave honestly even if others are cheating and that you go to God daily for guidance. But sharing your lifestyle can also be for a specific purpose. It can be to literally attract others to Christ and then to help your new friends make that step by inviting them to pray with you a prayer inviting Jesus into their hearts.

I believe this takes a while if it's done correctly. It's pretty rare when it makes sense to ask someone who's either a stranger or somebody you barely know to make such an important commitment. If you think about it, you really have to earn the right to talk about something so personal and so important. Otherwise, it might come across as trivializing the issue. ("Hi, let's talk. Do you know Jesus as your Lord and Saviour?") That approach does work for some people, but I think there are better ways.

So what I mean by earning the right is this: Get to know that unbelieving person over a period of time. Really become his or her friend (even if he or she doesn't become a Christian!). Genuinely care. Openly share your faith. And then (here's the most important part, so let's have a drumroll, please) ask the person directly whether he or she knows Christ. Offer to explain the Gospel. Tell how to take that step through prayer, and, if it seems appropriate, suggest praying the prayer together.

If you have the privilege of leading another person to the Lord in this manner, congratulations—you've just become an evangelist! Seriously, it's true. The work of evangelism today is being done by people just like you and me, folks who find a deliberate and intentional way to share their faith with another person for the express purpose of leading that person to a faith in Christ.

This means being on the lookout for people who God may have put in your path for this reason. This means living a life that will demonstrate the joy you have in your heart. This means finding an opportunity (plus the right time and place) to discuss the Source of your joy and then asking them if they want the same for themselves.

Obviously, this is a huge responsibility. It requires that our hearts are right with God first before we attempt to lead another to the Lord we profess to worship. If you have any doubts about this, I hope you will pray with me the prayer for today's meditation.

PRAYER:

Lord, today I give myself fully to You, even if I have made this commitment before. I do it today with a willing spirit. I ask You to forgive my sins. I promise to mold my life to be more like that of Your Son, whose life was sacrificed for mine. Thank You for the promise of salvation. Make me into the kind of person You can use today to draw others into a full relationship with You. Lead me to someone who needs to know You. Help me to establish a caring friendship with that unbelieving person. Give me the patience to establish a genuine relationship so that I have honestly earned the right to talk about You. Then, when the time and circumstances are right, provide me with the right words to help this seeker become a sincere believer. Amen.

62.

TODAY'S SCRIPTURE:

Meanwhile, the eleven disciples were on their way to Galilee, headed for the mountain Jesus had set for their reunion. The moment they saw him they worshiped him. Some, though, held back, not sure about worship, about risking themselves totally. Jesus, undeterred, went right ahead and gave his charge: "God authorized and commanded me to commission you: Go out and train everyone you meet, far and near, in this way of life, marking them by baptism in the threefold manner: Father, Son, and Holy Spirit. Then instruct them in the practice of all I have commanded you. I'll be with you as you do this, day after day, right up to the end of the age." (Matthew 28:16–20, The Message)

If I blew you away with the directness of yesterday's meditation, then please take time to meditate upon these words from today's Scripture.

Here we see that Jesus Himself commanded His people to go to those who do not know Him, to introduce them to the lifestyle of a loving and obedient relationship with Him and even to baptize these new believers in the names we call the Trinity (although these "names" describe one person in three beings).

This passage is known as the Great Commission, because Jesus "commissioned" His disciples (and us) to do this important work. People who understand military terminology (such as my two sisters, Stacey and Melissa—they both went to the Air Force Academy) can relate to what it means when we are commissioned. We are given the authority to lead. And, in the case of the Great Commission, this means "lead others to Christ." And this authority is what Jesus has given us and also asked of us.

Are you ready? Please spend the remainder of your meditation time today pondering this important question and praying to our Lord.

PRAYER:

Jesus, thank You for commissioning me to do this important work of telling others about Your sacrifice and inviting them to join Your family of believers. Please prepare me for a lifetime of service in fulfilling Your Great Commission. Amen.

63.

TODAY'S SCRIPTURE:

That if you confess with your mouth, "Jesus is Lord," and believe in your heart that God raised him from the dead, you will be saved. For it is with your heart that you believe and are justified, and it is with your mouth that you confess and are saved. As the Scripture says, "Anyone who trusts in him will never be put to shame." For there is no difference between Jew and Gentile—the same Lord is Lord of all and richly blesses all who call on him, for, "Everyone who calls on the name of the Lord will be saved." (Romans 10:9–13, NIV)

Today I am continuing on the theme of developing your evangelistic skills. Yesterday we also meditated on this important part of the Christian walk.

If you have the opportunity and privilege of telling another person about Christ, you may want to turn to this Scripture passage and show him or her the importance of "confessing with your mouth that you are saved." Some people think it's enough to love Jesus in their heart, but, according to the Bible, we are required to say that we are His.

Naturally, this means that once we have made such a declaration, we have told whoever heard us that we love Jesus, understand that He died for our sins and now live a new life. That puts us more or less in the public eye.

For you, it may mean showing your neighbor some kindness that is a result of your commitment to Christ. Maybe you bake her a cake and take it next door. Then, instead of just thrusting it into her hands, maybe you ask how her day is going and then really listen to her. Maybe that is the beginning of a friendship that will develop into an opportunity to pray with her for Christ to come into her life.

I believe this happens most effectively if, when you bring her the cake, you begin then by letting her know that you serve God. It's so easy to take the credit for a kindness. A neighbor opens her door and says, "Oh, how kind of you. I'm impressed by your baking skills!" But you can answer, "Well, I try to find time to do nice things for my neighbors because the Lord changed my heart from one of indifference to one of caring. So don't ever be impressed by me. It's God working through me." Naturally, these may not be the exact words you use, but you get the general idea. In fact, you may not be able to say something this direct so soon in the relationship. But from the beginning you need to establish humility and a commitment to something other than just impressing your neighbor with yourself.

So now you're in this person's life. In a way, this is being in the public eye.

As someone who has spent the last several years as a public figure, I can tell you that God will give you the strength to do this. It can be stressful at times, but He will make it possible if you ask Him.

And, just as you must ask Him into your heart as the initial step to becoming part of His family of believers, you must ask Him to guide you as you live your life openly for Him. If you have never done this, I hope you will join me in the following prayer.

PRAYER:

Dear God, I have taken the step of asking You into my heart. Now I want to live for You. And I want to show others that I belong to You. But there are so many pressures in my life. And a commitment to You means I have to make changes in my attitudes and behavior that others will see. Please give me the strength to live in this new way. Guide my activities, my conversations, even my thoughts as I spend today so that, if You put into my path a potential believer, I will be ready. Amen.

64.

TODAY'S SCRIPTURE:

. . . it is by grace you have been saved. (Ephesians 2:5, NIV)

As I told you in the beginning of this book, I am not a theologian nor a Bible scholar. But I can read (just as you can), and I can pass along my own experiences to you according to my understanding and daily attempts to live the Gospel of the New Testament.

So, with that caveat, I will try to describe what I think Paul meant in his letter to the Christians in Ephesus when he wrote that they had been saved by grace.

Author Scott Peck wrote in his book *The Road Less Traveled* that grace is when you're in a car accident and the car is crushed incredibly flat—like an aluminum can—and yet a space the shape of your body is left and a tiny air pocket remains to provide you with life.

In other words, grace is something that defies all logic. It describes a situation that shouldn't happen. And yet it does.

In the case of grace that saves your soul for eternity, it is a gift to you from God. But, because God is just and fair, it makes sense that we all should die without salvation. That's because we all have sinned and fall short of the glory of God, which means that—if the punishment fits the crime—then we should not have eternal life. Yet God grants it to His sons and daughters who understand that Jesus paid the price for us with His life.

Let's say that you commit murder, and the punishment for murder is death. So you go on trial and, sure enough, the jury finds you guilty. Then comes the sentencing. The judge tells you to stand so he can pronounce your sentence. You hold your breath waiting for him to say you must die in the electric chair or however your state performs an execution. But suddenly the judge turns to another man in the courtroom and says that man will die in your place. And now you're free to go. You don't have to be locked up another second. This man will lose his life because of your guilt.

That fictitious scene describes grace. And, although I say it's fiction because of the courtroom and the electric chair and all else that sounds like modern justice, it's actually quite close to the eternal truth of God's role as Judge.

I believe there are many people who think they become saved by their own actions. They think that because they take the step of saying "I believe in God," then God is so grateful for their commitment He says, "Then you can live for eternity with Me in heaven."

That's a little simplistic, in my opinion. That emphasizes our actions, rather than God's action of bestowing grace. And, most important, it doesn't even mention the role of Jesus, God's earthly Son, Who was sacrificed in our place to keep God's scales of justice perfectly balanced.

If you have never thought of this matter of grace, I encourage you to dwell on it in your meditation today.

PRAYER:

Dear God, You made the ultimate sacrifice for me by allowing Your Son to die in my place. It is almost impossible for me to completely understand this, but I am trying. Help me to comprehend "grace" by showing me other examples in my life. I will watch for them today. I want to grow in my understanding of You every day of my life. Amen.

65.

Now you, brothers, like Isaac, are children of promise. (Galatians 4:28, NIV)

Sometimes we Christians say we have been "born again." In fact, many people even make fun of this statement (they made fun of it in biblical days too, so we're in good company!).

There are many applications of this term, but there's one I particularly like. It refers to Isaac, the son of Abraham.

In Genesis we read that Abraham and his wife, Sarah, became the parents of Isaac when they were seemingly too old to have children. In other words, Isaac's conception and birth were miraculous—they were acts of God.

Then Abraham, who knew God intimately, was told by God to sacrifice his son Isaac. This meant Abraham was supposed to follow the custom of sacrifice as the Jews of those days did it—by using a lamb or other special animal. He took his son Isaac to a place where the sacrifice would be made. Isaac, of course, had no idea what was supposed to happen. In fact, in Genesis 22:7, Isaac even asks his father, "Where is the lamb for the burnt offering?" It is a very touching scene. The boy is so young and vulnerable. He trusts his father completely. How conflicted his father must have been to know that, in a few minutes, he would actually be killing his own son, especially since he was a child he and Sarah had waited so many years to have.

When the father and son reached the place where God had directed him to go, Abraham arranged an altar and placed wood on it. Then he bound up his son Isaac and laid him on the altar with the wood. He took out a knife to slay Isaac. Imagine how frantic Isaac must have been at this point and how heartbroken Abraham must have felt! Abraham was almost at the point of actually killing his son when God prevented it and assured Abraham that he would be blessed for this incredible show of obedience.

And so Isaac was saved. It was as though he was reborn. He had a second chance at life. It's even more meaningful because his *first* chance was a miracle too. (But then so is every birth, no matter what the age of our parents!)

When we accept Jesus as our Lord and Saviour by taking the time and giving the attention necessary to really comprehend what this enormous sacrifice of His life meant to us, then we have new life. It's like a rebirth. (If you are not sure what this sacrifice was, please reread previous meditations. Better yet, consult with a pastor.)

Have you been born again into the family of God?

PRAYER:

Lord, I accept Jesus as my Lord and Saviour. I am trying to comprehend what a sacrifice His death was to You and how important it is to me personally. This is a hard concept, but I commit to spending my life learning about it and appreciating it more every day. Thank You for leading me in this quest. Amen

66.

And so encourage one another and help one another, just as you are now doing. (I Thessalonians 5:11, The Good News Bible)

It may surprise you to learn that behind the scenes at the Miss America pageant not only are women primping like maniacs—they're also praying!

Naturally, we were in fierce competition with one another. The woman who wins Miss America statistically has competed with about eighty thousand women to achieve that title because of the large number of local and state contests held throughout the year. And, when the women arrive in Atlantic City, they size one another up and try to figure out who will get the best scores in all the categories.

When we dressed, the backstage area felt like a sorority house. You couldn't take a step without being zapped by some hair spray. Girls were climbing in and out of tiny swimsuits and huge gowns—all in the most cramped quarters you can imagine. We would borrow makeup and help with one anothers' hair. (I put makeup on a bruise on my thigh that resulted when I fell down during ballet practice.)

Because the atmosphere is so tense and frantic, the families of the contestants are housed at a different hotel from their daughters'. It makes sense, when you think about it. Imagine all those girls—plus mothers and sisters and aunts and grandmothers—backstage with eyeliner flying everywhere, and taffeta and shoes and petticoats and jewelry all over the place! What a circus that would be.

The year I was crowned Miss America I met about a dozen women who told me they follow Christ as their Lord and Saviour. And, in fact, we even had Bible studies during that final exciting week in Atlantic City. We prayed together and encouraged one another to accept whatever outcome was the result of the week of competition.

We could just as easily have spent the few spare minutes we had during that stressful week being catty—finding fault with this girl's nose, commenting about that girl's extra pound or two, whispering about someone's personality. And, if we had done so, that action could have crushed the spirit of a young woman who had her hopes so high (as we all did) for what would happen this week.

I'm not saying that those few of us who professed to be Christians never sinned or said unkind things or made terrible mistakes concerning others. But we made an attempt to encourage one another—instead of bringing our competitors down. And I think we often succeeded, because we sincerely tried.

Encouragement is so welcome in our high-stress world.

Who can you encourage today with an uplifting comment, a kindness, an offer of prayer?

PRAYER:

Lord, I will look for someone today to encourage. Help me find the right words for this person You may place in my path. Thank You for the words of encouragement You provide to me throughout Your Word, the Bible. Amen.

67.

Dear friends, since God so loved us, we also ought to love one another. (I John 4:11, NIV)

What I love about this verse—besides the message itself— is the way John writes "Dear friends."

Sometimes we take this business of friendship for granted. We enjoy the fun parts of it but we don't necessarily take responsibility for opportunities to be accountable to our friends.

People we know well, like our best friends, need to be reminded from time to time what is important in life. They need to hear us turn a frivolous conversation into a meaningful one. It's fun to laugh and joke, but it's also important to be serious.

By the way, just as we should admonish our friends (occasionally, not all the time, or they will get tired of us!), we should subject ourselves to the same from them. In other words, we should tell them that we welcome their help. We should state to our friends what are our goals and then we should feel obligated to live up to them.

This is called accountability. Many people are in accountability groups. They meet at intervals, such as once a week, and tell each other what are their goals. Then they report back the next week to tell what progress they've had in reaching those goals. Other people I know are in accountability relationships with another person, perhaps a best friend.

The most important accountability relationship, of course, is the one we have with God Himself.

PRAYER:

Dear God, I appreciate Your direction in every aspect of my life. Help me to gently guide my friends to look to You as I do. (I emphasize the "gently" part, Lord. I don't want to run my friends off!) Please introduce me to a person or group of people to whom I can be accountable. Amen.

68.

TODAY'S SCRIPTURE:

In your distress, when all these things have happened to you in time to come, you will return to the Lord your God and heed him.
(Deuteronomy 4:30, NRSV)

My wedding day, June 8, 1996, was a mixed blessing. I think many brides feel this way.

On the one hand, I felt incredible love for John. I know he is the man for me. Even though we occasionally argue, we always make up and affirm our love and commitment.

I also felt feminine and lovely in my white gown. Even though I had been privileged to wear many gowns during my reign as Miss America, there is nothing so beautiful as a wedding gown, and I cherish mine.

John looked handsome in his morning cutaway coat. It was a thrill to come down the aisle on the arm of my father and see the man who would become my husband in a matter of minutes waiting for me at the altar.

But other things about that day still haunt me. There

are some family hurts that have to heal. There are some unpleasantries that happen at times of stress. I know this often occurs around the time of a big family occasion like a wedding, and mine was no exception.

The important thing is that John and I were united in the presence of God. Sure, there was stress, but—just as this Scripture says—I believe we heeded the Lord. We knew we were meant to marry, and so we did.

The people who were with us that day were the ones who wanted to witness this holy occasion. And we cherish the gift of their presence and encouragement as we took this important first step in our lives together as husband and wife. I thank them now.

Are there people who were with you during a special occasion whom you should thank for "being there" for you?

PRAYER:

Father, forgive us for sometimes making happy occasions into stressful ones. Thank You for accepting us when we return to You and listen to Your voice. Amen.

69.

Jesus saith unto him, I am the way, the truth, and the life: no man cometh unto the Father, but by me. (John 14:6, KJV)

I promised to be truthful with my readers of this devotional book—including occasionally confronting you with what may seem to be a controversial truth.

Today's Scripture is the basis for the Christian religion and yet there are people who refuse to believe it.

We live in an age of tolerance. We tolerate people of other cultures and nationalities and even lifestyles. But many people interpret being tolerant to include tolerating a lax attitude toward this key verse. I believe it says very clearly that Jesus is the way to eternal salvation. If we do not believe this Scripture, then we must really ask ourselves if we believe *anything* in the Bible.

Personally, I don't think we are free to pick and choose which verses suit us and which don't. I believe all of Scripture was inspired by God and therefore is to be believed and followed.

I invite you to meditate on this truth today.

PRAYER:

Father, I know people of other faiths who I like, and so this verse is sometimes a bit hard to understand. I trust that You will show me its truth and make me comfortable with it as I learn more and more about how to live in Your will. Amen.

70.

TODAY'S SCRIPTURE:

And I say, "O that I had wings like a dove! . . ." (Psalm 55:6, NRSV)

I represent several organizations to raise money and awareness of issues about deafness. I travel a great deal and meet fascinating people.

One is a doctor named Bob Morris. He's doing research to help those with hearing disabilities, which affect 28 million people, making them the number-one disability in America. He gave me a treasure. It's a copy published by Doubleday, Doran & Company, Inc. in 1929 of Helen Keller's autobiography, *Midstream, My Later Life.*

His inscription is thrilling, but humbling, for me to read: "To Heather Whitestone, a woman from Alabama whose courage and perseverance mirror these qualities so remarkable in Helen's life. With best wishes, Bob Morris 2/9."

Naturally, Helen Keller is one of my heroines. Like me,

she had a mysterious illness when she was a toddler, but in her case it left her both deaf and blind. She wrote on page 248 that blindness was easier for her to deal with. She describes her correspondence with a French woman who was also deaf and blind. One thing which drew them together was their agreement that "we both feel the impediment of deafness far more keenly than that of blindness." But then, in typical Helen Keller form, her next sentence goes like this: "Both our lives have been made beautiful with affection and friendship."

It is so inspiring to me that she would describe her life as "beautiful." She was so accepting of her situation. All of us—me included—have so much to learn from her about gratitude!

PRAYER:
Lord, thank You not only for how You have made me but for the afflictions You allow. I will try harder today to be happy in my situation, whatever it is. Amen.

71.

Dear friends, now we are children of God, and what we will be has not yet been made known. But we know that when he appears, we shall be like him, for we shall see him as he is. Everyone who has this hope in him purifies himself, just as he is pure. (I John 3:2–3, NIV)

It's such a comfort to know that we will spend eternity with perfect bodies. We will not have hearing loss. No one will suffer from arthritis. People will not be worried about their weight. And on and on.

But why do we strive for such perfect bodies even while we are on earth? I think again today of Helen Keller, who wrote about being content with her multiple afflictions. She was so realistic about her limitations and yet she focused on what she *could* do, rather than what she could not do.

In her autobiography, *Midstream, My Later Life,* she talks about the proper role of ideals. On page 102 she quotes a man she knew who said: "Ideals are like stars—you cannot touch them with your fingers, but like the mariner on the desert of waters, you can follow them, and following come to port."

She put ideals in their proper perspective. They give us hope, something to reach for. But she knew not to expect perfection, at least on this side of heaven.

Helen Keller is one of the first people I will "look up" when I get to heaven. I want to sit at her feet and learn from her. How wonderful that both of us will be able to hear each other and she will be able to see!

PRAYER:
God, I'm grateful for the role models You sprinkle through my life. Your love and care is evident to me by who You put in my path. I pray that I will be a blessing to someone today. Amen.

72.

God's plan for the world stands up, all his designs are made to last. (Psalm 33:11, The Message)

The Lord is so faithful! He takes our problems and infirmities and uses them to His glory—if we will let Him.

Helen Keller was one person who allowed God to use her afflictions to demonstrate not only the excellence of the human will but also His power to overcome.

Because she was deaf, she didn't speak until she had been taught by her faithful teacher, Anne Sullivan. This bears some explanation. Deaf people, of course, have vocal cords. But it is hard to modulate a voice when you cannot hear the voices of other people. I know, because I have this problem too. And I can relate to Helen Keller's stories of fear as she stood before crowds of people to make a speech.

On page 97 of *Midstream, My Later Life,* she tells about her first terrifying public appearance after she had been prepped by her teachers:

"Oh, that first appearance in Montclair, New Jersey! Until my dying day I shall think of that stage as a pillory where I stood cold, riveted, trembling, voiceless. Words thronged to my lips, but no syllable could I utter. At last I forced a sound. It felt to me like a cannon going off, but they told me afterwards it was a mere whisper. . . . Everyone was kind and sympathetic, but I knew I had failed. All the eloquence which was to bring light to the blind lay crumpled at my feet. I came off the stage in despair, my face deluged with tears, my breast heaving with sobs, my whole body crying out, 'Oh, it is too difficult, too difficult, I cannot do the impossible.' But in a little while faith and hope and love came back and I returned to my practising."

What an inspiration to read of her courage. I too have been fearful as I've spoken all over the United States and in foreign countries.

Have you ever stood before a group of people and been afraid? I would be surprised if public speaking came easily to you! Very few people I know look forward to it.

Pray that God will give you the "faith and hope and love" that Helen Keller wrote about.

PRAYER:
Lord, when I am in a tense situation, I pray today that You will give me the faith, hope and love which I need to get me through. Amen.

73.

The night is nearly over; the day is almost here. So let us put aside the deeds of darkness and put on the armor of light. (Romans 13:12, NIV)

What I love about Helen Keller is that she was devoted to saving people from the darkness, not the darkness she suffered from as a blind person but the darkness of the spirit. She wanted people to experience the light of Jesus.

One of the most delightful parts of her book describe her visits with famous people like Alexander Graham Bell, Charlie Chaplin and Mark Twain (whose real name was Samuel Clemens). Her descriptions of a fond visit with Mr. Clemens at his Connecticut home reveal a warm friendship between two well-known people who truly enjoyed each other's company.

On page 66 of *Midstream, My Later Life*, she wrote: "I recall many talks with him about human affairs. He never made me feel that my opinions were worthless, as so many people do. He knew that we do not think with eyes and ears, and that our capacity for thought is not measured by five senses. He kept me always in mind while he talked, and he treated me like a competent human being. That is why I loved him."

As Mark Twain, the pen name Mr. Clemens used when he wrote such classics as *Tom Sawyer* and *Huckleberry Finn*, he was colorful, even vulgar in his choice of words. According to Helen Keller's book, he peppered his conversations with salty language. Yet she saw beyond that rough exterior.

As Christians, how often do we fail to overlook a personality that does not fit our image of acceptability? I'm sure I do this often, and if you also are guilty of this form of judgment, please pray with me the prayer below.

PRAYER:
Holy Father, I come to You with a heavy heart for the sin of judging others who may be colorful or full of fun to an extent which I think I cannot tolerate. Help me to see how great people like Helen Keller were able to overlook the faults of people and enjoy them for who they were. Amen.

74.

For God did not give us a spirit of timidity, but a spirit of power, of love and of self-discipline. (2 Timothy 1:7, NIV)

Even as she lived in a dark world with no sound, Helen Keller sensed a spirit within her.

Light in My Darkness, published in 1994 by Chrysalis Books, is a revision of Keller's book *My Religion,* which was published by Doubleday in 1927. Because her faith in God was such a driving force in her life, a revision of her old book seemed to be of interest to a public still hungry for an understanding of this remarkable woman.

Among the many lessons I learned from it is the confirmation that God places within us certain yearnings. For example, He gives us an innate desire to know Him. And, as today's Scripture passage points out, He gives us a spirit of power, of love and of self-discipline.

Helen Keller's life demonstrates this truth. For her first

six years, while she was trapped in a body that was like a silent, darkened tomb because she could not see or hear or speak, she still sensed *something*. Finally, a teacher was sent to her family's home in Alabama (my home state, by the way!). This woman reached Helen by pumping well water over her hand and then spelling the word *w-a-t-e-r* with an alphabet sign language. This simple act was the beginning of Helen's communication with the world.

Helen describes this event as the turning point for her. Suddenly, she understood that objects had names, and that someone was trying to tell her what they were. She was exuberant. Before that day, she had behaved almost like an animal, having temper tantrums, eating with her hands, being incorrigible, because she had no clear concept of the world around her and its social rules for living.

Now she was eager to learn. During the next few years Anne Sullivan opened up the world for Helen Keller. As the blind and deaf woman writes: "I noticed a difference between the way human beings did their work and the way the wonders of nature were wrought. I saw that puppies, flowers, stones, babies, and thunderstorms were not just put together as my mother mixed her hotcakes. There was an order and sequence of things in field and wood. . . ." (page 22, *Light in My Darkness*). Helen Keller was beginning to know God!

It is remarkable that she was not bitter toward the God

Who was slowly unfolding in her heart. I believe this is because He had given her a spirit of power, love and self-discipline.

When people say they don't believe in God, I think of this lesson from her book. Often people who claim to be nonbelievers say they have no evidence that God exists. Yet they have not searched their own hearts. The Christian faith teaches that we all have the capability to know God, because of the way He has made us.

As Helen herself put it on page 12: ". . . there is still in the lowliest of men and women something called faith, which will respond to those speaking with the greatest of all authority, the authority of an inward conviction of the truth of God's message."

PRAYER:
Heavenly Father, thank You for giving me a spirit of power, of love and of self-discipline. This tells me You created me to know You. And this convinces me that You created me to belong to You. I pledge today to better understand this concept and to seek You in everything I do. Amen.

75.

But when the Friend comes, the Spirit of the Truth, he will take you by the hand and guide you into all the truth there is. (John 16:13, The Message)

If you will indulge me one more lesson for us to meditate on from the life of Helen Keller, then I promise to turn to another subject after this.

She was just so remarkable to me and I hope to you!

This is how Helen describes her "spiritual awakening," according to *Light in My Darkness,* page 25:

I had been sitting quietly in the library for half an hour. I turned to my teacher and said, "Such a strange thing has happened! I have been far away all this time, and I haven't left the room."

"What do you mean, Helen?" she asked, surprised.

"Why," I cried, "I have been in Athens!"

Scarcely were the words out of my mouth when a

bright, amazing realization seemed to catch my mind and set it ablaze. I perceived the realness of my soul and its sheer independence of all conditions of place and body. It was clear to me that it was because I was a spirit that I had so vividly "seen" and felt a place thousands of miles away. Space was nothing to spirit! In that new consciousness shone the presence of God, who is a spirit everywhere at once, the Creator dwelling in all the universe simultaneously.

The fact that my small soul could reach out over continents and seas to Greece, despite a blind, deaf, and stumbling body, sent another exulting emotion rushing over me. I had broken through my limitations and found in the sense of touch an eye. I could read the thoughts of wise men and women—thoughts that had for ages survived their mortal life—and could possess them as part of myself.

If this were true, how much more could God, the uncircumscribed spirit, cancel the harms of nature—accident, pain, destruction—and reach out to his children! Deafness and blindness, then, were of no real account. They were to be relegated to the outer circle of my life. Of course I did not sense any such process with my child-mind; but I did know that I, the real I, could leave the library and visit any place I wanted to, mentally, and I was happy. That was the little seed from which grew my interest in spiritual subjects.

And, dear readers, I can echo what Helen Keller says about how a disability—such as mine, deafness—can be relegated to the outer circle of my life because it is of no real account. What is "of account," however, is the Lord's presence at the center of my life. And I hope and pray He is at the center of yours.

PRAYER:
Lord, thank You for giving us people like Helen Keller to demonstrate Your faithfulness and also to provide insight into the indomitable human will, which You have created in all of us. This study has been a blessing to me. Your presence is evident in her life, because you planted in her a desire to know You and then You built on that seed with levels of understanding. Please do the same for me. I want to uncover layers and layers of knowledge about You so I can grow as close as possible. I yearn to know You better. Open my eyes and ears today to Your eternal truth. Amen.

76.

"Come, follow me," Jesus said, "and I will make you fishers of men." (Matthew 4:19, NIV)

Even several years after my reign as Miss America 1995, people still send me fan mail. In fact, I get it every day, and it touches me greatly. I try to respond to as much of it as I can.

Most letters are from girls and women. But one day recently I opened my mail and found a wonderful note from a man. He included a lapel pin with the American sign language symbol for "I love you" (index and little finger up, thumb extended, other two fingers tucked into the palm). Superimposed onto the cutout of the hand was the Christian fish symbol, which has become an outward sign of being a Christian. Combined, the two images provide a powerful yet simple reminder of Christ's call to us to love one another.

This man wrote me that he is a special education

teacher who uses sign language with his multi-disabled children. So he was glad to have me speak up for this misunderstood group. He wrote: "It is wonderful to see a celebrity express their love of God openly throughout their daily public lives."

I pray that other celebrities will feel comfortable telling the public about their faith. I believe we are entering a time when more and more will realize their potential as witnesses for God's grace.

If you know of a celebrity who is a Christian and openly discusses it in public, please write to him or her and provide encouragement. It shouldn't be such a tough public stand to take, but, for many celebrities who are believers, it is. I believe your expressed appreciation for them will help.

PRAYER:

Lord, make me Your instrument. When people need encouragement, give me the courage to speak up. I want to follow Jesus and be a "fisher of men." Amen.

77.

. . . But as for me and my house, we will serve the Lord. (Joshua 24:15, KJV)

"You served your crown well and used it for the glory of the Lord. What a wonderful God we serve!" When these words tumbled out of a recent fan letter, I thought, Yes! We do serve a wonderful Lord. And yes! She realized that I wore the Miss America crown not for myself but to glorify the Lord. It is gratifying to know that so many of my fans have figured this out.

In the case of this particular writer, she had an incredible story to tell. She had lost both her mother and her father within a few weeks of each other. Their deaths occurred about three months before the Miss America pageant on September 17, 1994, when I was named winner of the title for the following year.

She wrote that she had watched the television broadcast of the pageant. And, the moment when she heard my name announced as the new Miss America, it was the first time she had smiled since the deaths of her parents. She smiled because she herself is a Christian, and she knew I would be open about my faith as I traveled as Miss America.

Although I'm sure my winning did not dig her out of an understandable depression, it is a pleasure to know that it caused her to smile that night.

By the way, this fan tucked a special present into her letter: a cross-stitching of the Joshua verse I used as today's Scripture.

PRAYER:
Thank You, Lord, for allowing us to smile even at a time of deep grief. Thank You for using us to cheer up another person. Please place someone in my path today to lift up in Your name. Amen.

78.

Better a meal of vegetables where there is love than a fattened calf with hatred. (Proverbs 15:17, NIV)

To me this proverb means that the simple things of life, when sprinkled with love, can be far better than what the world often considers to be great.

To illustrate I'll share two stories about my dogs—my chocolate Lab, Graham, and my bulldog, Mack.

One night I couldn't sleep because I felt ill. Quietly I slipped into the bathroom with pillow and blanket and lay on the floor in case I became sick to my stomach. As much as I tried not to wake anyone, in a few minutes in came John and Graham. They snuggled up with me right there on the floor, and I felt better just having them near. When I did become sick, Graham looked sad, putting his sweet head down on his front paws and giving me what I call a mercy look. John made me smile despite my upset stomach. Their love was the medicine I needed.

On another occasion John and I had a little fight. I did not like the way he had treated me, so I went upstairs. John came up and apologized, then asked me for a kiss. Still mad, I picked up Mack and held him to John's face. The dog gave John a sloppy kiss, but it was just the kind of icebreaker John and I needed to begin making up. Again, one of God's creatures interjected love and reminded me of the importance of what we sometimes take for granted.

PRAYER:

Lord, I appreciate all that You have given me, including even my pet dogs. I recognize that You are the source of everything that is good, and today I take the time to acknowledge it. Thank You for shaping my heart to understand and enjoy what You have created to please me. Amen.

79.

The tongue that brings healing is a tree of life, but a deceitful tongue crushes the spirit. (Proverbs 15:4, NIV)

Do you have a teacher who influenced your life so much that you remember her (or him) to this day, no matter what your age?

This meditation is dedicated to our wonderful teachers, and it includes another true confession from me of a time when I said something that was very insensitive.

My education included public schools in Alabama and a school for deaf children in St. Louis, Missouri. Frankly, being with other deaf kids was a wonderful experience. I gained confidence in myself and trust in others. I also was a better student during that time because the classes were so small. For example, the ratio was usually one teacher for every three students, so there was a great deal of individual attention.

I became accustomed to this favorable ratio. When I

returned to Alabama and went back into the school system with hearing kids, I had an adjustment to make.

One day a teacher stopped me as I was leaving the classroom and asked how she was doing as far as I was concerned. In other words, my teacher was asking me for a report card on her work!

Well, I'm a little ashamed to admit this but, thinking of the favorable ratio I enjoyed in St. Louis, I replied negatively to the teacher, who was trying to reach both her hearing students and me, a deaf one. Later, when I realized how my harsh comment probably discouraged her, I went back and apologized.

The older I get, the more I realize the importance of "minding our tongues." We can use them for harm or we can use them for the glory of God. How will you use yours today?

PRAYER:

Dear God, give me the discernment today to know what to say to the people I talk to. Help me choose my words carefully. Guide my comments. Make me accountable for everything that comes out of my mouth. I want to please You in all that I do. Amen.

80.

TODAY'S SCRIPTURE:
Therefore God has mercy on whom he wants to have mercy, and he hardens whom he wants to harden. (Romans 9:18, NIV)

I'm saddened to think how many people don't realize that God is in control of all that happens. Throughout the Bible we see evidence of this.

In the Book of Job, we see God giving Satan permission to make attacks on a man, Job, who is known to be righteous because he fears the Lord and shuns evil. In a conversation with God, Satan expresses his desire to test someone, and God offers to this fallen angel His servant Job. I admit that this is as hard for me to understand as it probably is for you, and yet I have to accept that it is accurate, because I believe the Bible is true. By the way, this story has a wonderful ending, with Job "passing the test" and being rewarded generously by God. But the point I am making is that this situation was completely under God's control.

In the Book of Exodus we read that God hardened

Pharaoh's heart. The king of Egypt did not respond to Moses' many requests to "let my people go." Moses demonstrated God's power to Pharaoh. Yet, the king remained stubborn and firm. Over and over we read verses saying that God hardened Pharaoh's heart. Again, this is difficult for us to understand, but it proves to me that God is always in control.

If you doubt God's power, I invite you today to meditate on this Scripture and truth.

PRAYER:

Father, You are in control of everything. As a mere human being, this is difficult for me to comprehend. But I accept this truth, because I know Your Creation is for my own good. Thank You for Your wisdom in all matters. Amen.

81.

TODAY'S SCRIPTURE:
*Now the serpent was more subtile than any beast of the field
which the Lord God had made. And he said unto the woman, Yea,
hath God said, Ye shall not eat of every tree of the garden?
(Genesis 3:1, KJV)*

Obedience is one of the hardest lessons to learn.

Many people think that God's admonition to Adam
and Eve not to eat the fruit from a certain tree in the
Garden of Eden was simply a mean show of power. It is
hard for people to accept that, as our Heavenly Father, God
has reasons for telling us what to do and what not to do.

Someone speculated that maybe the reason behind this
"rule" which God gave to Adam and Eve was to keep them
in the dark about certain information. This idea stems, I
think, from the fact that the tree was called "the tree of
knowledge." In other words, some people think God was
simply trying to keep Adam and Eve at an unfair advantage,
keeping them stupid, so to speak.

What a misunderstanding of how our Heavenly Father deals with us!

We sometimes apply this same thinking to our parents. I cannot count the number of times I thought my parents were being unreasonable when they gave me limits. Now that I'm older I realize these were for my own good. I can accept these limits better now that I'm a woman in my twenties thinking about having children of my own someday.

This is how I now understand the passage about not eating fruit from this certain tree. I believe it was God's way of introducing to Adam and Eve the lifelong habit of discernment based on God's direction. Although they were adults, they were learning from Him like children. This was God's loving way of teaching them about a pattern they would need forever: trusting God, depending on Him and applying their own discernment based on what He taught them.

PRAYER:
Heavenly Father, thank You for loving me enough to give me limits. Because of Your care, I can better understand my parents. Amen.

82.

TODAY'S SCRIPTURE:

Meanwhile, Saul was still breathing out murderous threats against the Lord's disciples. He went to the high priest and asked him for letters to the synagogues in Damascus, so that if he found any there who belonged to the Way, whether men or women, he might take them as prisoners to Jerusalem. As he neared Damascus on his journey, suddenly a light from heaven flashed around him. He fell to the ground and heard a voice say to him, "Saul, Saul, why do you persecute me?" "Who are you, Lord?" Saul asked. "I am Jesus, who you are persecuting," he replied. "Now get up and go into the city, and you will be told what you must do." (Acts 9:1–6, NIV)

The story of Paul's conversion is very dramatic. Even many nonbelievers know the story of the man whose name had been Saul. He persecuted everyone who called Jesus the Messiah. But one day he was on the road to the city of Damascus. He was struck by a heavenly light. And he had an encounter with Jesus Himself. This event completely

220

turned his life around. His rebirth as a believer even included a new name, Paul.

One of the many ironies about Paul, who wrote much of the New Testament, is that he became the object of much persecution. He received thirty-nine lashes on five occasions because he refused to deny that Jesus was his Lord and Saviour. Paul also was stoned once, beaten with rods three times and almost lost his life in shipwrecks on three occasions. Yet, he did not lose heart. Even when he was imprisoned and abused in ways no one should ever have to endure, Paul remained faithful to Christ.

It's difficult for us in the modern world to imagine such hardship. I know there are countries where brutality is still common, and occasionally we even hear about it happening here in the United States. But, truthfully, how many of us could endure such suffering for our Lord?

Even that strong saint of a woman, Mother Teresa, did not go through physical abuse, although she denied herself the creature comforts we take for granted. She endured a great deal in the name of Jesus, and, by doing so, she accomplished so much.

I'm always a little hurt when I hear radical feminists dismissing Paul as a woman-hater. This is such a misunderstanding! It's an example of someone being quoted out of context and unfairly interpreted.

Paul admired women and included them in his ministry. I remember one passage in which he arrived to preach a sermon and his only listeners turned out to be women. The custom of that day would have allowed him to simply turn away, to "cancel his appearance," so to speak. Women had so little clout in the culture that, without losing the respect of those in authority, Paul easily could have dismissed the idea of speaking to them. However, he didn't. He conducted the meeting exactly as he would have if he had been speaking to a group of men. I admire him for that. Paul was human, but he was one of the strongest men in the Bible.

PRAYER:
Thank You, God, for Paul. He is a true role model for manhood. You preserved the story of his conversion to influence us, and You preserved his writings to guide us. I appreciate Your loving-kindness by giving us this man to know. Amen.

83.

Then the disciples went back to their homes, but Mary stood outside the tomb crying. As she wept, she bent over to look into the tomb and saw two angels in white, seated where Jesus' body had been, one at the head and the other at the foot. They asked her, "Woman, why are you crying?" "They have taken my Lord away," she said, "and I don't know where they have put him." At this, she turned around and saw Jesus standing there, but she did not realize that it was Jesus. "Woman," he said, "why are you crying? Who is it you are looking for?" Thinking he was the gardener, she said, "Sir, if you have carried him away, tell me where you have put him, and I will get him." Jesus said to her, "Mary." She turned toward him and cried out in Aramaic, "Rabboni!" (which means Teacher). Jesus said, "Do not hold on to me, for I have not yet returned to the Father. Go instead to my brothers and tell them, 'I am returning to my Father and your Father, to my God and your God.'" Mary Magdalene went to the disciples with the news: "I have seen the Lord!" And she told them that he had said these things to her. (John 20:10–18, NIV)

In this book we have meditated for the past several days on God's power to control all situations and also the important role of women in doing God's work.

Today I draw your attention to this vital passage from the Gospel of John. I cannot think of one that is more instructive in drawing together these points. You will recognize it as being one of the stories often read on Easter Sunday. And that's because it *is* the Easter story. It is the moment when Jesus first appeared after His excruciating death on the cross as the risen and resurrected Lord and Saviour. And, as Christians, it is this truth and reality upon which we base our faith.

In the version of the Bible I used for today's Scripture, the words of Jesus appear in red ink. This helps the reader to know—even before it dawns on Mary—that the man actually is Jesus, whom she is mistaking for a gardener (because she was standing near his tomb, which was located in a garden).

So very many sermons have been preached on this passage that I know all I can add is my perspective as a believer who is tremendously moved every time I study it. I see something new with each reading. And, because this story is the foundation of Christian belief in Jesus as the Messiah, I invite you to read it closely and, of course, prayerfully. Ask the Holy Spirit to open your eyes to truths in this passage that you have never seen before today.

Here are three thoughts from my own notes:

First, Jesus chose to reveal Himself (in his resurrected state) to a woman. In fact, it's interesting to note that she was a woman who had been a prostitute. But He loved her unconditionally. Mary became a follower of His after she repented, accepted Him as the Messiah and changed her ways. Obviously, Jesus (who was actually God in human flesh) could have orchestrated this encounter near the tomb any way He chose. He certainly knew the long-term consequences. He knew the moment would be recorded for all the world to read in a book we know today as the Bible. He could have made sure it was a *man* who was there and not a woman, if He thought this would make a greater impact. I'm convinced this is one of the greatest clues we have to the fact that God loves and honors women.

Second, it is obvious from this passage that God gives women a great deal of responsibility. Mary is the one who is sent to the "brothers" (disciples) to report what she had seen and heard. Obviously, if Jesus thought that she, as a woman, would not have credibility, then He would have sent a man. And, in the culture of that day, when women were held in low regard, that would have been an option. However, as usual defying traditional culture in favor of His own perfect way, Jesus chose to send a woman for this important task of testifying to His risen state. In addition, it is significant that He sent someone who had been known as a sinner, which demonstrates how thorough is His forgiveness.

Third, this passage reminds us that, if we do not expect to see Jesus, then we might not recognize Him. It is interesting that Mary was looking directly at Him, and yet she did not immediately know Who He was. People have speculated that maybe He was standing in the shadows or His face was partially covered by the hood of His robe. All of that may be true. But I think the lesson is still this: *We must expect to find Jesus.*

There are many more lessons I have learned from this passage over the years, and I'm sure you have your lessons as well. Whether mine are new to you or not, I invite you to ask God to place in your heart what He wants you to learn from Mary's encounter with the risen Lord on the day we now call Easter.

PRAYER:

Today, Lord, I will expect to find Your risen Son, Jesus. I will look for Him in my life. I ask You to plant this expectation in my heart, so I will be alert as I go about my daily tasks. I do not want to miss this most important of all encounters. Amen.

84.

And there was a certain royal official whose son lay sick at Capernaum. When this man heard that Jesus had arrived in Galilee from Judea, he went to him and begged him to come and heal his son, who was close to death. "Unless you people see miraculous signs and wonders," Jesus told him, "you will never believe." The royal official said, "Sir, come down before my child dies." Jesus replied, "You may go. Your son will live." The man took Jesus at his word and departed. While he was still on the way, his servants met him with the news that his boy was living. When he inquired as to the time when his son got better, they said to him, "The fever left him yesterday at the seventh hour." Then the father realized that this was the exact time at which Jesus had said to him, "Your son will live." So he and all his household believed. (John 4:46–53, NIV)

How much we are like the royal official in this passage! We have to see Jesus' miracles to believe in them.

What I think is often overlooked about this passage, however, is that the man "crossed over" to demonstrate his

227

faith. In other words, he apparently worked for King Herod, who certainly was not Jesus' ally. But this man was not only so desperate to save his son's life but also so trusting of Jesus that he risked his job and reputation by believing. And he was rewarded with the miracle of healing.

Do we trust Jesus enough to make such a public proclamation?

PRAYER:

Jesus, I have heard of "foxhole believers," people who believe in You only when they are in a desperate situation. I pray that my faith will be steady and even, that I will trust You even when times are good. Help me to follow this path of faith. Amen.

85.

TODAY'S SCRIPTURE:

Have mercy on me, O God, according to your unfailing love; according to your great compassion blot out my transgressions. Wash away all my iniquity and cleanse me from my sin. For I know my transgressions, and my sin is always before me. Against you only have I sinned and done what is evil in your sight, so that you are proved right when you speak and justified when you judge. (Psalm 51:1–4, NIV)

It is my understanding that Psalm 51 was written by David when he was out of fellowship with God.

The occasion was after his adulterous affair with Bathsheba and then his murderous abuse of power as king by ordering that her husband be killed on the battlefield. Later, when he and Bathsheba had a son together, that son died, and David recognized that his death was the consequence of his sinful behavior.

Sin, of course, does have consequences. We have seen this in our own national leaders.

David is known as a man "after God's own heart," which means that he understood God and was greatly favored by God. It is hard to understand how a man with such promise and potential could stoop so low. And yet we still see this happening today.

In this psalm, David admits that he has sinned, he expresses sorrow and then he eventually vows to change his behavior and to walk again with the Lord.

In verse 10, he writes a line that is used in one of contemporary Christian music's most popular praise songs: "Create in me a pure heart, O God, and renew a steadfast spirit within me."

How honestly do we admit the connection between sin and its consequences?

PRAYER:
O God, I come to You, as David came, with contrition in my heart for sins I have committed. I ask You to create in me a pure heart and renew a steadfast spirit within me. Thank You for Your generous forgiveness. I pray that today I will be more mindful of the consequences of sin. Amen.

86.

To all God's beloved in Rome, who are called to be saints: Grace to you and peace from God our Father and the Lord Jesus Christ. (Romans 1:7, NRSV)

If you were raised in a faith tradition that freely uses the word "saint," then this passage may bring to mind people anointed and elevated throughout centuries to that revered title.

As for myself, two modern-day people come to mind: Mother Teresa and Billy Graham.

Mother Teresa was flesh and blood, just like you and me, and yet she walked so closely with the Lord that she achieved special status. She devoted her life to living for the Lord in a public way. All this is true, too, of Billy Graham. I cannot think of two people in this century who deserve our respect more.

Mother Teresa devoted her life to the poor children of Calcutta, India. She also spoke out on many other issues, as the Holy Spirit led her. Even when she was old and frail, she traveled to address large assemblies of people. She spoke at the annual Congressional Prayer Breakfast in Washington, D.C., and urged the president to ban abortions.

Billy Graham has led thousands, perhaps millions to a saving faith in Jesus Christ through his revivals and his organization, which provides help to anyone seeking to know the Lord and make a commitment to Him.

But are these the only people who can be considered "saints"?

A closer inspection of this Scripture reveals that Paul specifically calls *all of us* to be saints. Does this lower the status of this special term? No, I think it inspires us to reach higher, to be challenged to live our lives in a more deliberate way, to be more open about our faith so that others will see Christ through us.

Do you?

PRAYER:

Lord, I want to be like Your Son, Jesus. I know this is a big ambition but I see that Paul called the Christian citizens of Rome "saints." And I want to reach to this status too, not for my glory but for Yours. Amen.

87.

TODAY'S SCRIPTURE:

But Ruth said, "Do not press me to leave you or to turn back from following you! Where you go, I will go; Where you lodge, I will lodge; your people shall be my people, and your God my God." (Ruth 1:16, NRSV)

The story of Ruth and Naomi gives us a model for the proper daughter-in-law to mother-in-law relationship.

First, Naomi showed courage by serving God, even while she was living in a foreign land. She had lost her husband and her two sons to death, and yet she was not bitter. She chose to return to her homeland of Judah. She released her daughters-in-law to flee back to their own people and their own gods. Orpah took her mother-in-law up on the opportunity, but Ruth stayed behind in this remarkable show of loyalty.

Ruth was rewarded with a new husband in Boaz. Her loyalty to Naomi is what attracted this "man of standing" to her. He told her in Ruth 3:11: "All my fellow townsmen know that you are a woman of noble character." The result of their union was a son named Obed, who was the father of Jesse, who in turn was the father of David. Thus, Naomi, who had lost her sons and the opportunity for heirs with their death, becomes connected to the line of David, which also makes her related to Jesus.

So not only does the relationship of these two women teach us about loyalty, it also demonstrates that achieving the kingdom of God is decided not by blood and birth, but by the conformity of a person's life to the will of God.

PRAYER:

Lord God, teach me to respect my elders as Ruth treated her mother-in-law, Naomi. Thank You for these role models, who show us the way to You and the way to live in Your family. Amen.

88.

TODAY'S SCRIPTURE:

But the woman had taken the two men and hidden them. She said, "Yes, the men came to me, but I did not know where they had come from. At dusk, when it was time to close the city gate, the men left. I don't know which way they went. Go after them quickly. You may catch up with them." (But she had taken them up to the roof and hidden them under the stalks of flax she had laid out on the roof.) So the men set out in pursuit of the spies on the road that leads to the fords of the Jordan, and as soon as the pursuers had gone out, the gate was shut. (Joshua 2:4–7, NIV)

The story of Rahab, the prostitute who helped the Israelites in Jericho, is one of the most heart-warming examples in the Bible of how God uses all kinds of people to accomplish His goal.

Anyone who thinks "I am not worthy" or "I don't have the right kind of training" should read this fascinating account.

Rahab went by her instincts (women's intuition?) and

hid the Israelite spies, who were looking over the Promised Land before bringing the people across the Jordan River to settle there. These spies were "wanted men" (their posters were on the post office wall!).

But Rahab courageously hid them and aided their spying. She became a convert to the God of Israel and a famous woman among the Hebrews.

In fact, she is listed at the beginning of the Book of Matthew among the ancestors of Jesus!

PRAYER:

Lord, give me the courage of ordinary people like Rahab. She did not let her station in life keep her from helping Your cause, and You honored her by making her part of the lineage of my Lord and Saviour, Your Son, Jesus. She is another heroine whose potential You wisely recognized. Amen.

89.

How the mighty have fallen in the midst of the battle! Jonathan lies slain upon your high places. I am distressed for you, my brother Jonathan; greatly beloved were you to me; your love to me was wonderful, passing the love of women. (2 Samuel 1:25–26, NRSV)

The story of the three generations of kings—Saul, David and then Solomon—is rich with love, madness, deceit, wisdom and many other human characteristics.

One of the most touching relationships in this long saga is the bond between two good friends, Jonathan, son of Saul, and David, who would become king.

At one point in the story Saul becomes a paranoid madman, chasing David everywhere in his effort to kill him. David could barely stay ahead of Saul and, in fact, several times was close to being captured or slain. Their chase would make an exciting movie!

Jonathan also could have been in pursuit of David. As the king's son, he had every reason to believe he should become king. However, he and David shared a special understanding of the Lord's will. They knew that the Lord had handpicked David to become king, and Jonathan was humble enough to accept this and also loyal enough to David to step out of the way.

We rarely see friendships like this anymore. Groups like Promise Keepers are promoting solid, godly friendships, but I would like to see more men help each other to fulfill their destinies rather than be competitive. I think this would be a wonderful contribution to society by the Christian community.

Can you find a way to encourage two men to be supportive of each other?

PRAYER:
Lord, I praise You for planning our lives. If only we will listen to Your plans! I would like to be an encouragement to people—men, in particular—who want to be supportive of each other rather than competitive. Please find a way to use me in this way if it is Your will. Amen.

90.

TODAY'S SCRIPTURE:

In the same way instruct the older women to behave as women should who live a holy life. They must not be slanderers or slaves to wine. They must teach what is good, in order to train the younger women to love their husbands and children, to be self-controlled and pure, and to be good housewives who submit themselves to their husbands, so that no one will speak evil of the message that comes from God. (Titus 2:3–5, The Good News Bible)

Yesterday we discussed how men can support one another rather than be competitive.

Women can do the same thing by encouraging one another with mentoring friendships. Older women can be an example to younger women, teaching them the godly ways to be wives, mothers and—in our society—even career women.

In this passage we see God's plan for role models between women of various ages. What women must do is to follow this example with mentoring programs in their churches or simply by taking it upon themselves to pair up with other women and enter into such a commitment.

A woman in Florida credits the survival of her marriage to her godly relationship with an older woman. Another one in Massachusetts says her mentor got her through a terrible struggle when her mother died. Still a third woman in Arizona says the year she spent in a formalized relationship with another woman based on Titus 2 helped with her career planning.

Is there a woman in your life who you could pair up with for a relationship like this?

PRAYER:

I come to You, Father, with a promise to live by Your Word, the Bible. You instruct us to encourage one another. If it is Your will for me to be in a relationship like the one described in Titus 2, please lead me to such a woman. Amen.

91.

TODAY'S SCRIPTURE:

Blessed is the country with God for God; blessed are the people he's put in his will. (Psalm 33:12, The Message)

People like to argue whether America's founders were truly believers in God who were also Christians.

I accept that it is debatable to what extent each of them was a devotee of the faith. However, I truly believe that we were founded on Christian principles and that God Himself favors the success of America. This seems obvious to me when reading speeches and documents written at the time the patriots were planning the revolution and laying the foundation for a new nation.

By the same token, I think God must be very frustrated with us as a nation as we degenerate into moral decay with drug use, rampant crime, abortions and people out of control in every generation.

The version I have chosen of today's Scripture uses the term "will." Other versions, such as the New International

Version, the one I have used most often throughout these meditations, uses "inheritance." Both mean that which God gives to us as His children, passes along to His heirs.

Is the country we have inherited still reflecting godly principles? I think not. Can you do anything about it? I challenge you to spend your meditation time today reflecting on ways that you can contribute to this country through your prayers, your activism or your voice.

PRAYER:
Lord, thank You for the nation You have given to us. I am afraid we are failing to live by Your principles. If you see a role for me in turning this around, please steer me in that direction. I will watch today for an opportunity from You to be a godly citizen. Amen.

92.

Therefore, since we are surrounded by such a great cloud of witnesses, let us throw off everything that hinders and the sin that so easily entangles, and let us run with perseverance the race marked out for us. Let us fix our eyes on Jesus, the author and perfecter of our faith, who for the joy set before him endured the cross, scorning its shame, and sat down at the right hand of the throne of God. Consider him who endured such opposition from sinful men, so that you will not grow weary and lose heart. (Hebrews 12:1–3, NIV)

For me this is one of the most uplifting Scripture passages in the Bible.

It brings to my mind a group of people running in a carefree manner with the wind in their hair. They know that the race is a righteous one because it is for the Lord. Although they are in competition, they are also trying for what athletes call their personal best—the new time that breaks their old record. Ahead of them they see the cross.

The vision of it in front of them energizes them to run as hard as possible, to do their best.

Yet these runners are not trying to beat each other in the classic sense. They are not trying to win so that others will lose. Their success will not be at the expense of the other runners. No, in their race, everyone can win! For in this race, the definition of success is to throw off sin, to leave it behind, to successfully outrun it.

I see these runners with big smiles on their faces. They will finish. They will win. All of them.

PRAYER:

Lord, thank You for providing us with not only a race to run but a worthwhile cause. The cross is a great incentive to do our best in Your name. Today I will run for You as hard as I can. Amen.

93.

Then Caleb silenced the people before Moses and said, "We should go up and take possession of the land, for we can certainly do it." But the men who had gone up with him said, "We can't attack those people; they are stronger than we are." And they spread among the Israelites a bad report about the land they had explored. They said, "The land we explored devours those living in it. All the people we saw there are of great size. We saw the Nephilim there (the descendants of Anak come from the Nephilim). We seemed like grasshoppers in our own eyes, and we looked the same to them."
(Numbers 13:31–33, NIV)

Today's Scripture passage amuses me because I can relate to it. First, I will give you the background of the biblical story.

The Hebrews had been wandering in the desert following their exodus from Egypt, where they had been slaves to Pharaoh, the king. Moses had led them out of Egypt, delivering them through the Red Sea as God miraculously

245

parted it, leaving a dry path for them to follow. Then Moses delivered to them the Ten Commandments written on two tablets. These were God's rules to them for worshiping Him and getting along with one another in a civil society.

So after a year in the desert the people were ready to enter the Promised Land, which they considered to be a "land of milk and honey"—in other words, rich in natural resources, so they could make a good living and start their lives there.

But during their wandering the people grumbled and became disgruntled. Their views of reality were distorted, because they had been isolated and had fallen into some sinful ways.

So Joshua and Caleb headed an expedition of men. They acted as spies to check out the Promised Land (today known mostly as Israel) before the large band of Hebrews crossed the rivers and valleys and settled there.

After their forty-day expedition, the men returned and gave their report to Moses and Aaron.

Caleb, as the passage shows, was unafraid of the people they saw. He was confident not only in their ability to conquer the territory but in their God, Who would protect them. His report was based on faith in the God Who had protected them and gotten them this far.

But how quickly the other men had forgotten the miracles they had experienced during what was only their first year in the desert!

When the others on the expedition spoke up, they said they felt inferior to the people they saw. They described themselves as "grasshoppers" compared to the men who already populated the Promised Land. They allowed the negative self-image that troubles many of us to intimidate them. They focused on their fear rather than on God.

How many times have we felt we had to conquer giants—and that we were simply puny insects compared to our adversaries? Yet, if the mission we are pursuing is a godly mission, if it is for God's kingdom and not done just for our personal glory, then how, ultimately, can we fail?

Oh, sure, it may be hard at first. In fact, there may be serious setbacks. Any missionary can tell you how difficult it is to establish a foothold in a pagan society or community. But our God is bigger than *any* adversary. No "giant" is bigger than He is.

If you size up a situation before you charge in—as Joshua and Caleb were asked to do—I hope you will factor in whether God is on your side.

PRAYER:
Father, I have a full day today. I will deal with people who support me, but I also will encounter some obstacles. Remind me that You are by my side in all that I do, if it

247

glorifies You. Give me a realistic point of view. I am not asking to be puffed up with false pride because I belong to You. That, too, would be wrong. I am asking for the confidence to know that You will be with me today and every day. I know that I serve a God Who can conquer all. Amen.

94.

Don't use bad language. Say only what is good and helpful to those you are talking to, and what will give them a blessing. (Ephesians 4:29, The Living Bible)

Does bad language shock you? Probably not, because we hear so much of it these days. Television and movies are full of four-letter words—language that can't be printed in most magazines and newspapers but which can invade our homes through TV or seem to assault us when we go to theaters. In fact, even so-called family movies often include words that very few parents will let their kids utter (or, if they do, I think they're pretty lax disciplinarians).

The Bible is clear about this practice. God tells us not to use bad language (the New International Version says "do not let any unwholesome talk come out of your mouth"). Not only is it offensive, it is a sloppy way to talk. People who resort to swearing are taking the lazy way out of communicating. It's disrespectful to their listener, even if the listener is participating too (in other words, they're dragging each other down into the gutter if they're *both* doing it!).

Many people, even Christians, I'm sorry to say, think bad language is harmless. What's worse, they sometimes think it's cool.

But God asks us to set ourselves apart from people who are not believers, the "world." And one of the ways we can do this is by cleaning up our language. This includes avoiding even those words and expressions that are substitutes for bad words (surely, you know what I mean!). Using substitute words is better, but it still calls to mind the words you are replacing.

Please join me in working to set this higher standard.

PRAYER:
Lord, I ask You to make me accountable for the language that comes out of my mouth. I want my words to glorify You, not shame You. It's one of the ways I want to show others that I belong to You. Amen.

95.

TODAY'S SCRIPTURE:

Ask and it will be given to you; seek and you will find; knock and the door will be opened to you. For everyone who asks receives; he who seeks finds; and to him who knocks, the door will be opened. (Matthew 7:7–8, NIV)

A fan told me this wonderful story. It illustrates how God delights in answering our prayers.

A book signing was being held in my honor. I was invited to sit at a special table in a bookstore and autograph copies of my first book, *Listening with My Heart* (Doubleday, 1997). The book is my autobiography.

One woman desperately wanted to buy a copy and have it signed by me, but she couldn't afford it. She was going through hard times financially. But her heart was overflowing with a desire to read my story, to learn how God has worked in my life.

She prayed for God to come up with a solution. She knew His promise: ask, seek, find.

A few days before my appearance she was wandering through a yard sale. Suddenly, she spied a copy of my book. She discovered the price—only 25 cents! This was amazing—a hardcover book for only a quarter. And the very book she had prayed to receive!

When the woman showed up at the book signing and told me her story, I was thrilled for her.

I love this story not only because it tells how God keeps His promises, it demonstrates how a faithful follower can "ask, seek and find."

PRAYER:
Nothing is impossible for You, Lord. I will watch for someone today to tell about Your wonders! Amen.

96.

TODAY'S SCRIPTURE:

So I say, live by the Spirit, and you will not gratify the desires of the sinful nature. For the sinful nature desires what is contrary to the Spirit, and the Spirit what is contrary to the sinful nature. They are in conflict with each other, so that you do not do what you want. But if you are led by the Spirit, you are not under law. The acts of the sinful nature are obvious: sexual immorality, impurity and debauchery; idolatry and witchcraft; hatred, discord, jealousy, fits of rage, selfish ambition, dissensions, factions and envy; drunkenness, orgies, and the like. I warn you, as I did before, that those who live like this will not inherit the kingdom of God. But the fruit of the Spirit is love, joy, peace, patience, kindness, goodness, faithfulness, gentleness and self-control. Against such things there is no law. Those who belong to Christ Jesus have crucified the sinful nature with its passions and desires. Since we live by the Spirit, let us keep in step with the Spirit. Let us not become conceited, provoking and envying each other. (Galatians 5:16–26, NIV)

These straightforward words from the Book of Galatians tell us what to do and what not to do. They list sinful acts. And if you think you can get away with doing these, then what do you suppose God means by saying: "those who live like this will not inherit the kingdom of God"?

If God is the Author of the Bible (which I believe to be true because of historical and archaeological evidence and also the faith in my heart), then He means business!

By the same token, God lists the qualities that prove a person is filled with the Holy Spirit. These are called "fruits of the Holy Spirit," because they are the products of a life lived in response to Him and made possible through the indwelling of the Holy Spirit. These are: love, joy, peace, patience, kindness, goodness, faithfulness, gentleness and self-control.

Do the characteristics on either of these lists describe you?

PRAYER:
Lord Jesus, I declare today that I belong to You. I pray that I have crucified my sinful nature with its passions and desires. Help me to produce the harvest of fruits that come from a life spent following You and responding to Your Holy Spirit, which You so generously filled me with when I became Your child. Amen.

97.

TODAY'S SCRIPTURE:

For you created my inmost being; you knit me together in my mother's womb. I praise you because I am fearfully and wonderfully made; your works are wonderful, I know that full well. My frame was not hidden from you when I was made in the secret place. When I was woven together in the depths of the earth, your eyes saw my unformed body. All the days ordained for me were written in your book before one of them came to be. (Psalm 139:13–16, NIV)

One of the ugliest words in our language is "holocaust." Literally, it means "a large-scale destruction of life." Generally, this horrible word refers to the Holocaust of World War II, when six million Jews and other people were killed by Nazis, who were carrying out the orders of a madman, Adolf Hitler.

You may be wondering where I am going with this. The Holocaust, after all, is a terrible thing to think about. People were murdered, and they died excruciating deaths.

I'm mentioning it because I believe there's a holocaust

going on in America today in the form of abortions. At least twenty-five million babies have been murdered since the passage of *Roe* v. *Wade* in 1973. This murderous act can be committed anytime during the pregnancy. It is legal in America to kill a baby that is on the way down the birth canal and is only seconds from a natural delivery. We have a policy known as "abortion on demand."

And yet when I read verses like the ones in Psalm 139, I realize that God literally knit each of us together in our mother's womb. How can we be so arrogant as to decide who among us should live and who should die—all in the name of our convenience?

I know that an unwanted pregnancy must be an unhappy situation. But I also know that people grow from adversity. I became deaf, and I believe I am a better person today because I grew from that adversity. People overcome their problems with God's help. Many people find God for the first time because of difficulties they suffer. And God certainly looks after His own. It is true that many children suffer because of bad situations, but I believe God uses even the most oppressive circumstances to reveal Himself. The reason for allowing such suffering may take years to unfold. In fact, the truth may not be discovered until we meet God and ask Him.

Surely, God does not take lightly our irresponsibility and lack of appreciation for His creation, His intentionally knitting together a baby in the mother's womb! He has done this great and miraculous act for a reason. He has a plan for that child. He does not create any human being for us to reject. He creates a baby for us to care for. The baby belongs to Him and is simply "on loan" to us. It is our privilege to raise and look after that baby throughout childhood and then into adulthood—all on behalf of God.

When I look carefully at this verse, I am overwhelmed by the beauty of God's act of creation, not only creation of all of nature but the creation of us as His people.

And I sense the incredible tenderness with which He made each of us. He carefully selected every detail that makes us who we are. God loves us so much!

If you agree with me on this vital issue—the holocaust of our country—please join me in speaking out. I know that God must grieve every time a child of His dies, especially at the hands of a mother.

God created us with His gentle, loving hands for a purpose. It is our job to discover His plan for our life. And it is our privilege to glorify Him in all that we do.

PRAYER:
Heavenly Father, thank You for the gift of life. Forgive me when I defile that gift by abusing my body or even by hurting another person in any way. Please give me courage if I am ever faced with a situation, such as an unwanted

pregnancy, from which I am tempted to run. Show me the path to dependence on You in such circumstances. I trust that You will lead and guide me through any trauma which You allow to happen to me—just as You lovingly carry me on Your strong, broad shoulders every day of my life. Amen.

98.

TODAY'S SCRIPTURE:

I am not saying this because I am in need, for I have learned to be content whatever the circumstances. I know what it is to be in need, and I know what it is to have plenty. I have learned the secret of being content in any and every situation, whether well fed or hungry, whether living in plenty or in want. I can do everything through him who gives me strength. (Philippians 4:11–13, NIV)

By now you have learned a lot about me, including anecdotes from my life, my opinions on cultural issues, my reasons for admiring certain people, my thoughts on how to live a life that reflects Christ.

As I promised you in the beginning of this book of meditations, I would be completely honest. And I have been—even when I was afraid I might be going too far!

I hope that these ninety-nine meditations introduce you to a lifestyle of going daily to God, reading His Word in the Bible, meditating on its application and praying with a thankful heart that asks for and expects His guidance.

I'm concluding with a poem I wrote during a lengthy airplane ride. I titled it "A Poem of Jesus' Bride":

As I wander at the beach,
You surprise me with Your sparkling water like a
    diamond,
With breezes on my face.
You unveil my hair with Your strong, yet gentle hands.
The seagulls ring the bells with their voices,
And the waves applaud as You say, "Arise, my love
    and come with me."

Then night falls, as the stars play the harps for Your
    romance.
The moon lights a candle in Your chamber.
The breeze smooths my face, bringing Your fragrance.
You draw me into Your mysterious, yet loving spirit.

The diamond still sparkles
But no longer can hold Your overflowing love.
As the diamond spills more love onto the sand,
Your heart shines through my body onto little
    miracles.

Suddenly I remember where I came from.
Here I lie down in Your beautiful chamber as a bride,
Who does not wish to go back to her world.

I look up at the gentle stars,
Thinking this will not last longer.
Your kiss fills my heart with sweet wine.

Then the warm waves rub my feet,
Encouraging me to look down.
There You show me how beautiful a bride I am in
    Your eyes.
And, as the stars sparkle on my head,
You crown me with Your praise and everlasting life.
I am the bride of the Mighty King of all kings.

—Heather Whitestone McCallum

PRAYER:
Thank You, Lord, for loving me unconditionally. Amen.